A TREASURY OF
CLASSICAL GUITAR
REPERTOIRE

Cover photo by Robert Amft

ISBN 978-0-634-08912-1

Visit Hal Leonard Online at
www.halleonard.com

World headquarters, contact:
Hal Leonard
7777 West Bluemound Road
Milwaukee, WI 53213
Email: info@halleonard.com

In Europe, contact:
Hal Leonard Europe Limited
1 Red Place
London, W1K 6PL
Email: info@halleonardeurope.com

In Australia, contact:
Hal Leonard Australia Pty. Ltd.
4 Lentara Court
Cheltenham, Victoria, 3192 Australia
Email: info@halleonard.com.au

Adelita
(Mazurka)

Francisco Tárrega

Allegro Spiritoso

Mauro Giuliani

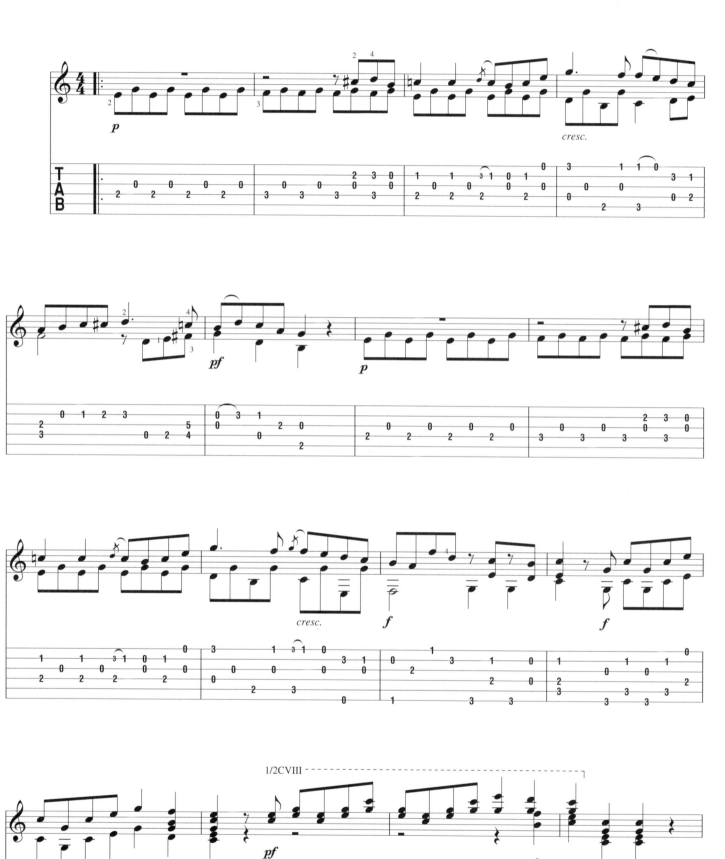

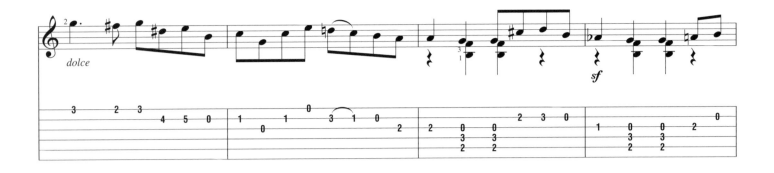

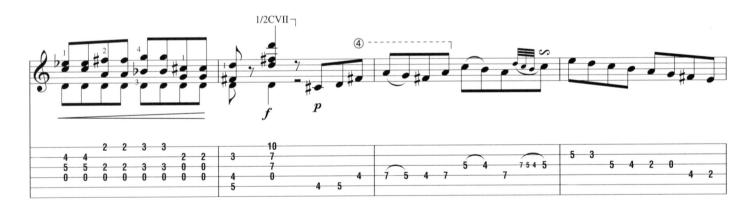

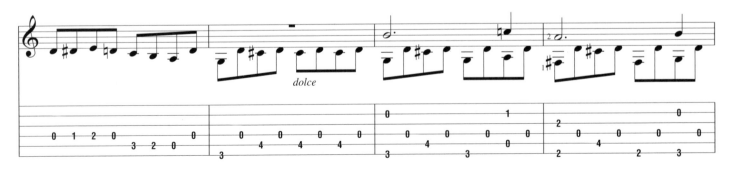

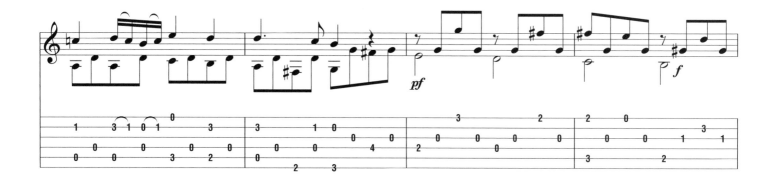

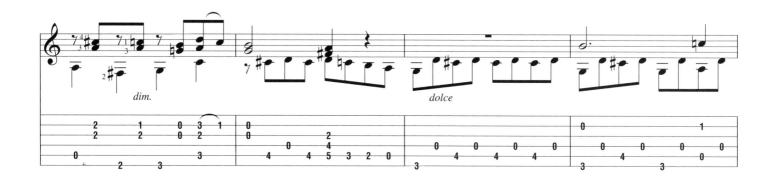

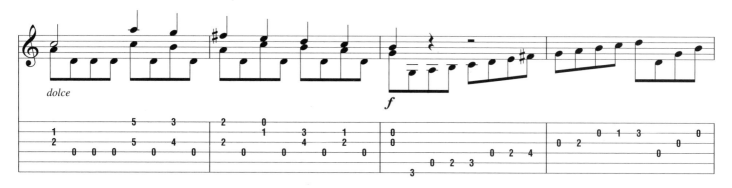

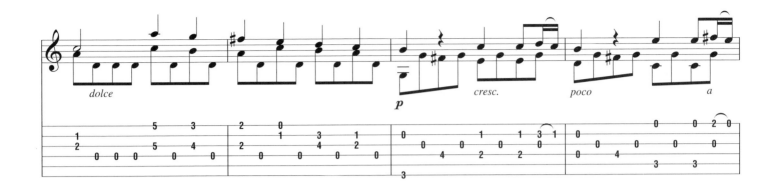

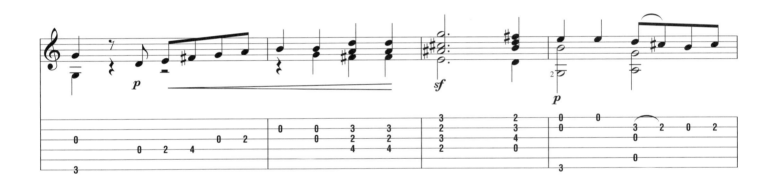

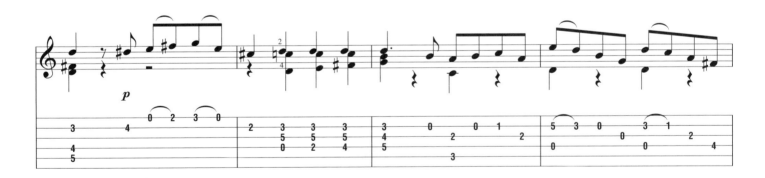

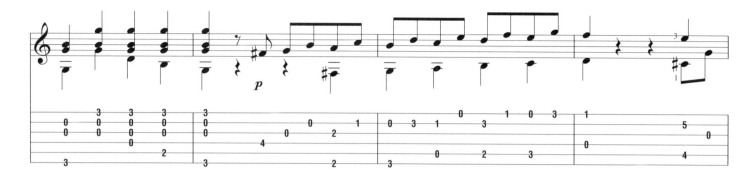

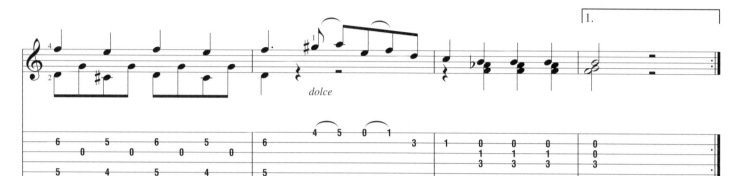

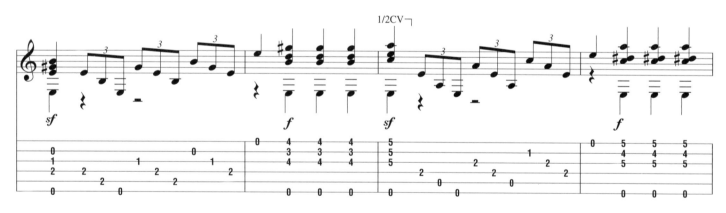

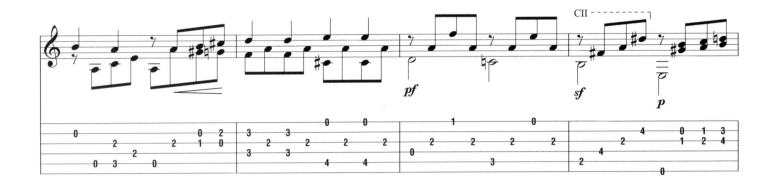

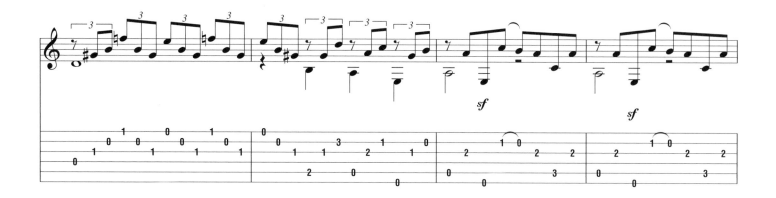

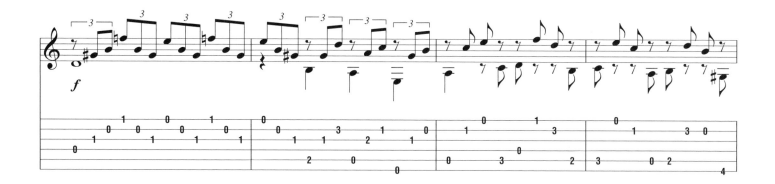

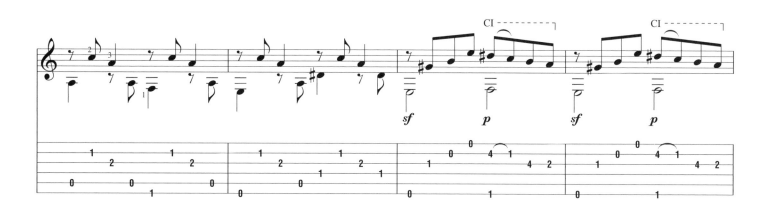

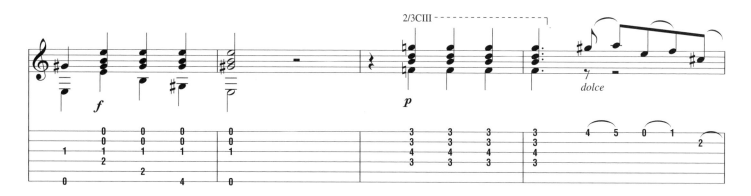

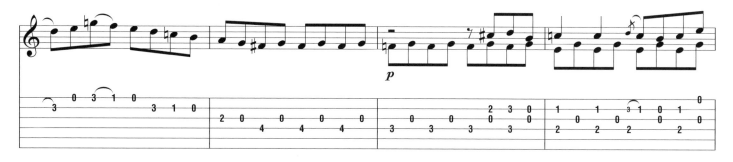

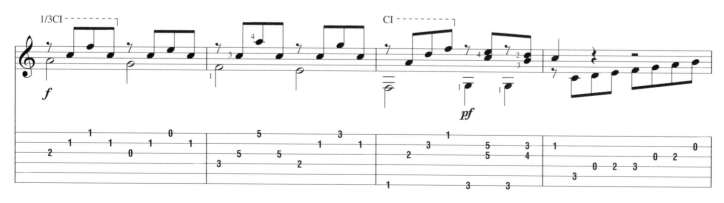

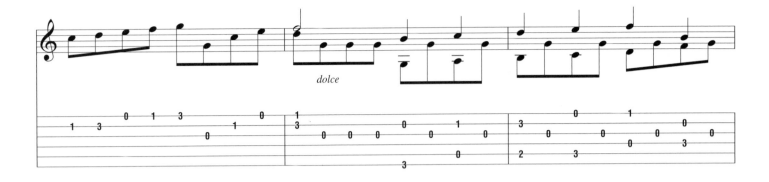

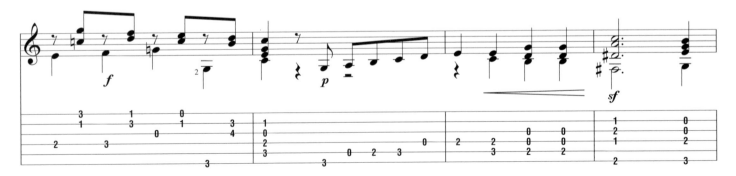

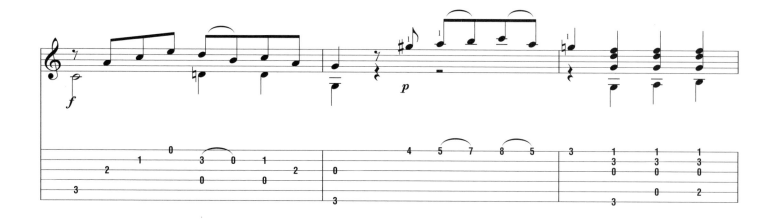

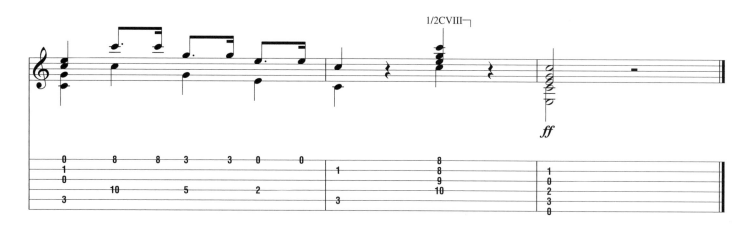

Bianco Fiore

Cesare Negri

Tuning:
(low to high) D-A-D-G-B-E

Bourrée

Robert de Visee

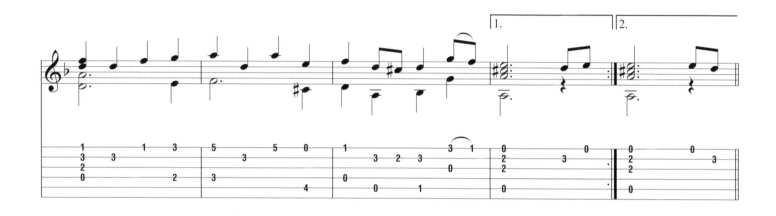

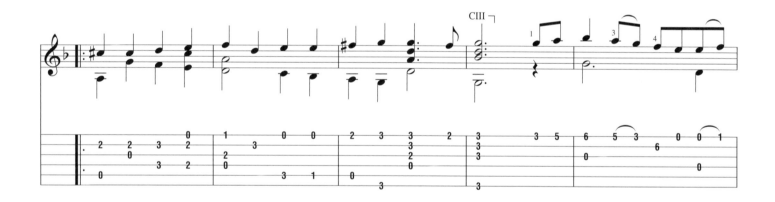

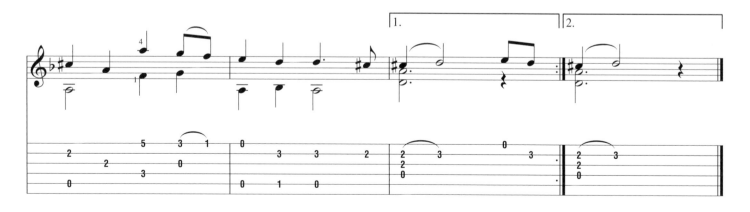

Bourrée in E Minor

Johann Sebastian Bach

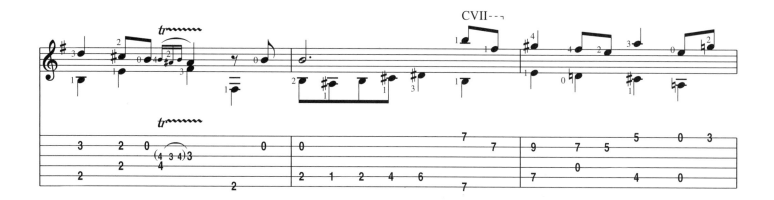

Capriccio

Johann Anton Logy

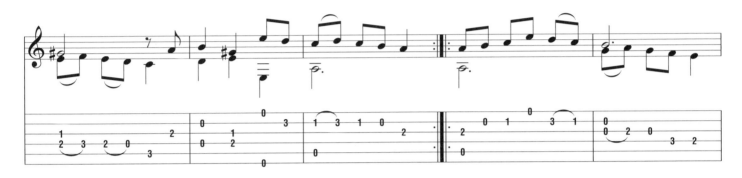

Dowland's Galliard

John Dowland

Captain Digorie Piper's Galliard

John Dowland

Tuning:
(low to high) D-A-D-G-B-E

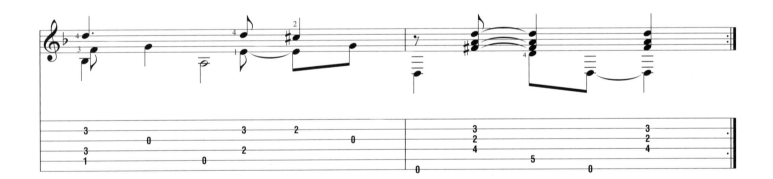

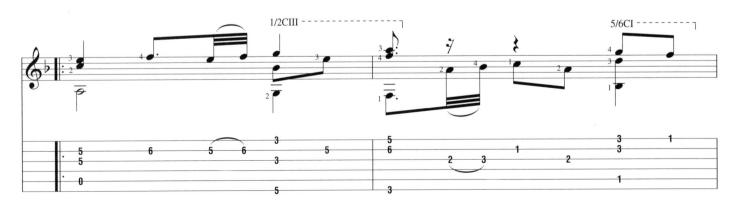

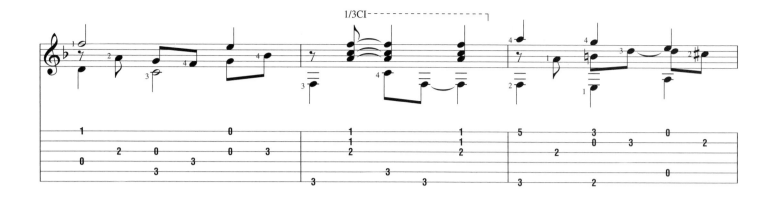

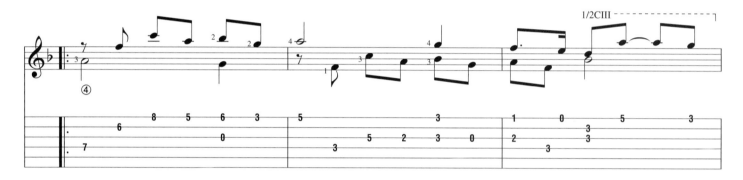

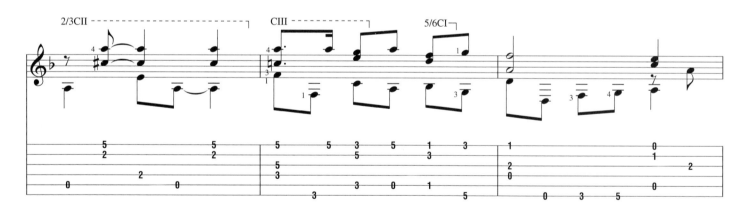

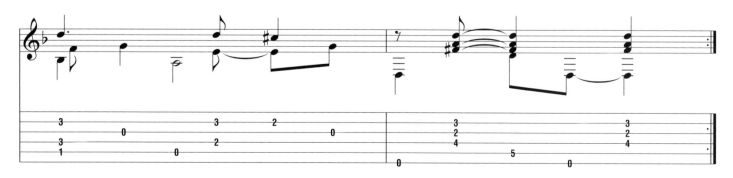

Españoleta

Gaspar Sanz

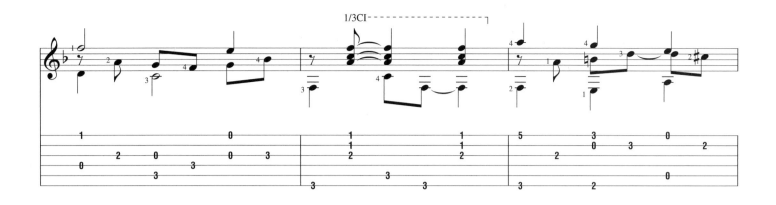

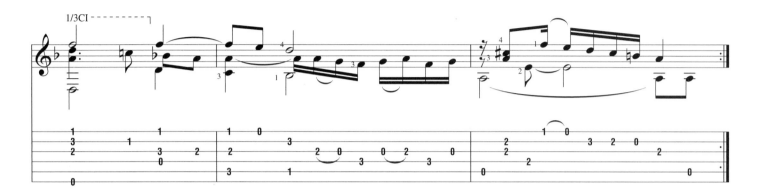

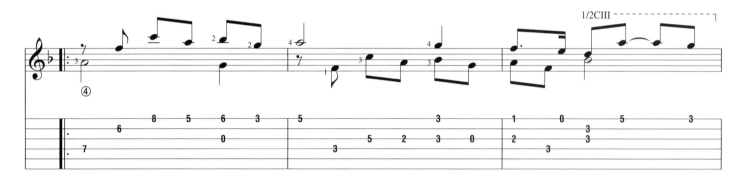

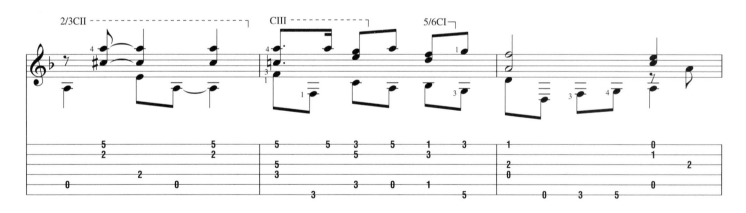

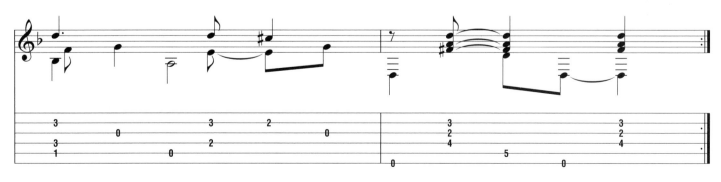

Españoleta

Gaspar Sanz

Estudio

Francisco Tárrega

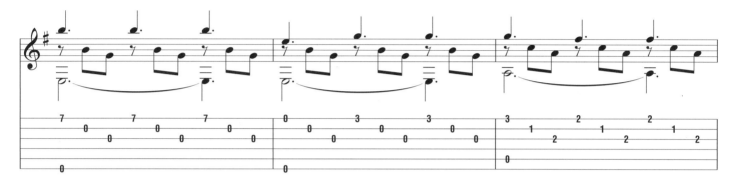

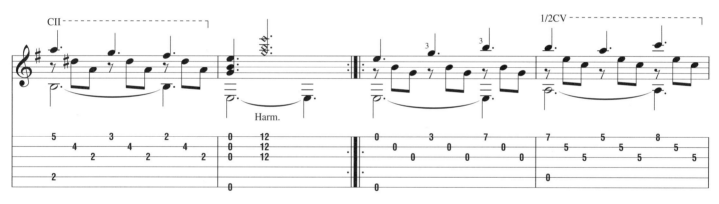

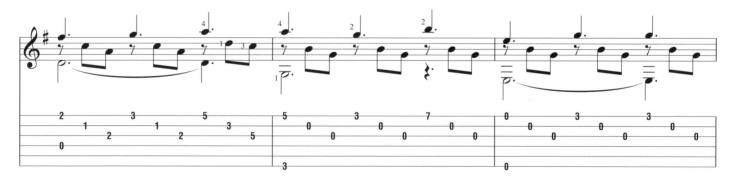

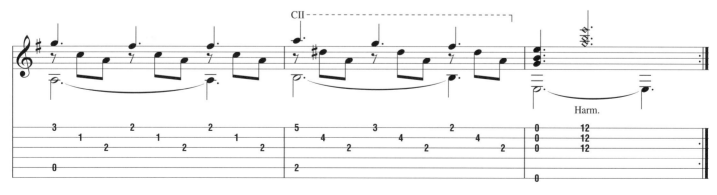

Etude in E Minor

Mauro Giuliani

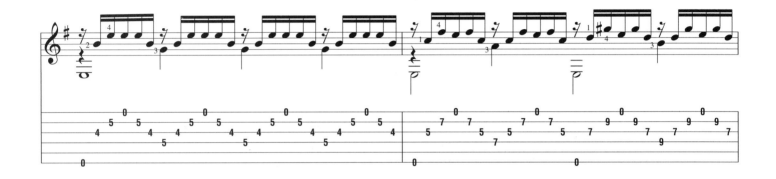

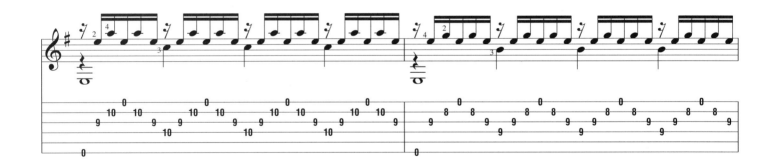

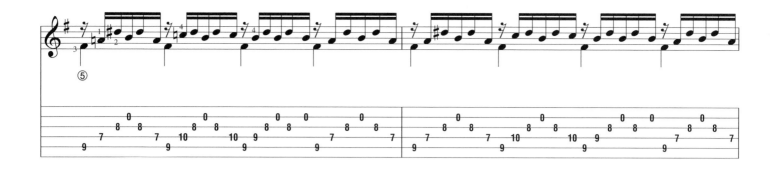

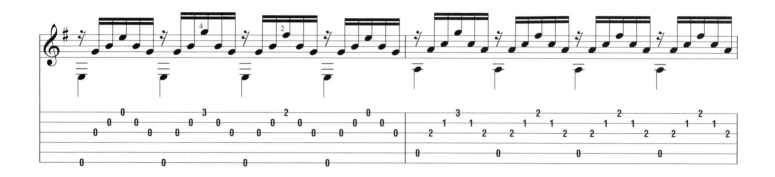

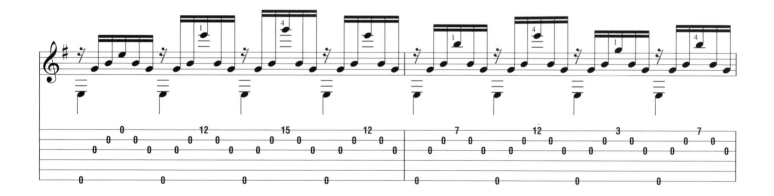

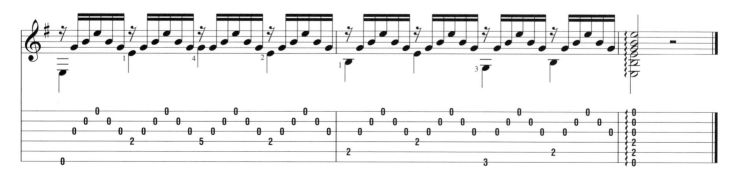

Gavotte I & II
from *The 6th Cello Suite*

Johann Sebastian Bach

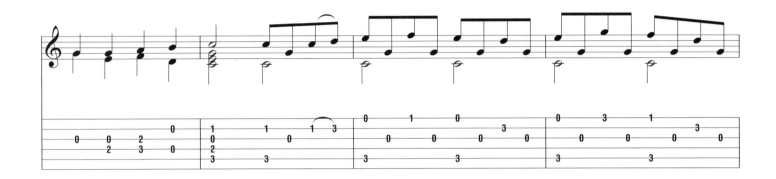

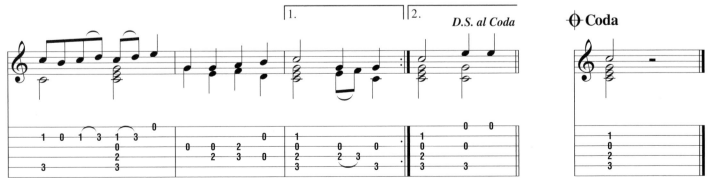

1.

2. *D.S. al Coda*

 Coda

Greensleeves

Sixteenth Century Traditional English

Gigue

Johann Anton Logy

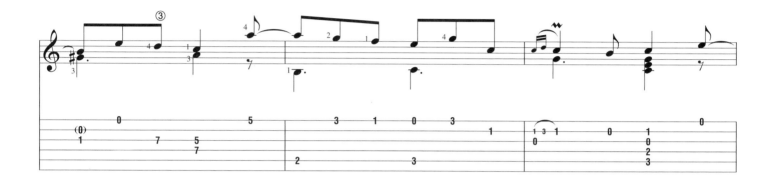

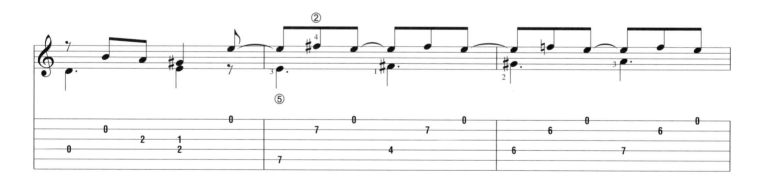

Gigue

Robert de Visee

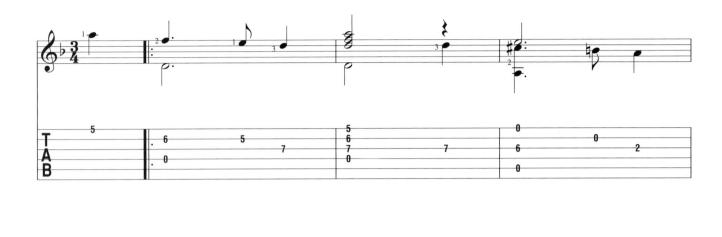

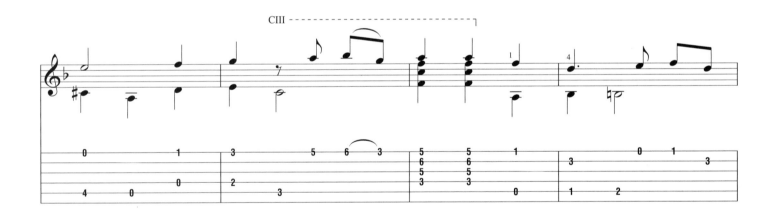

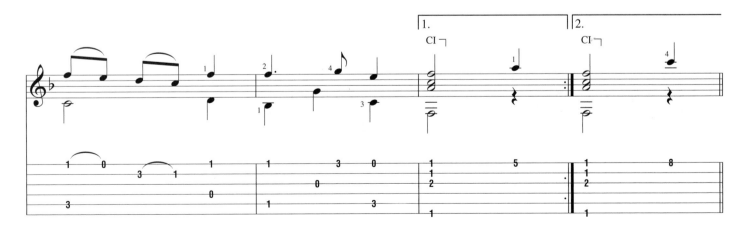

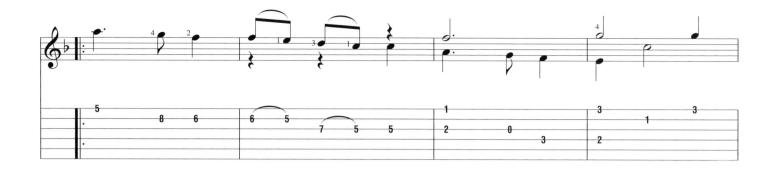

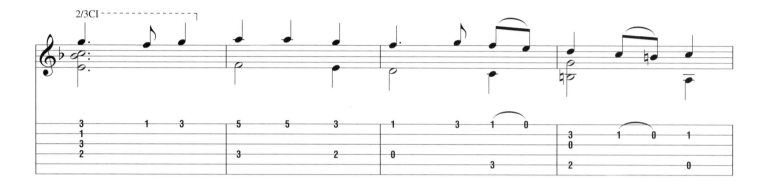

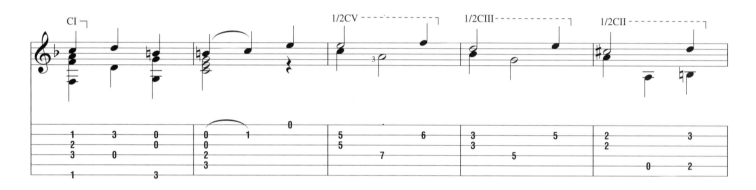

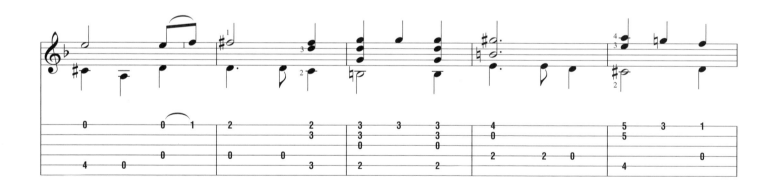

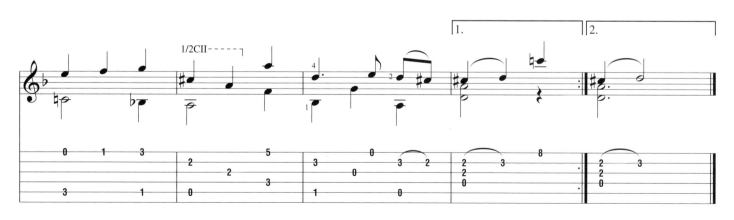

Gymnopedie No. 1

Erik Satie

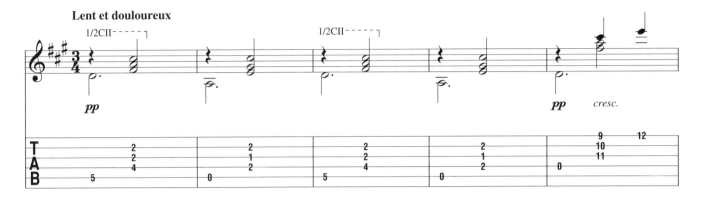

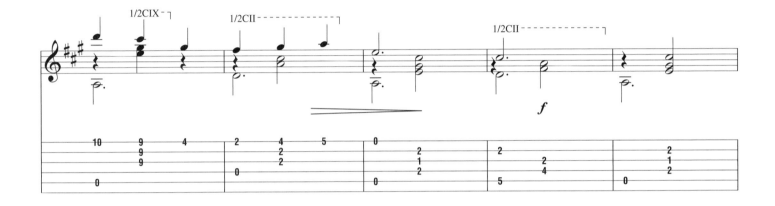

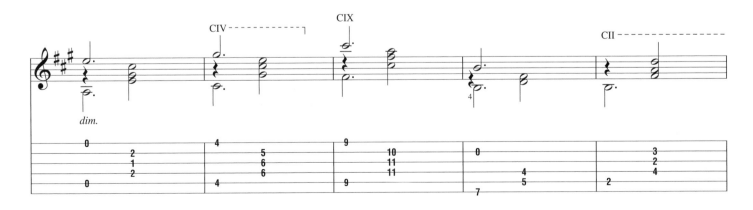

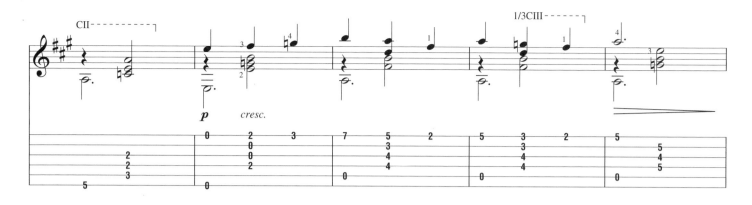

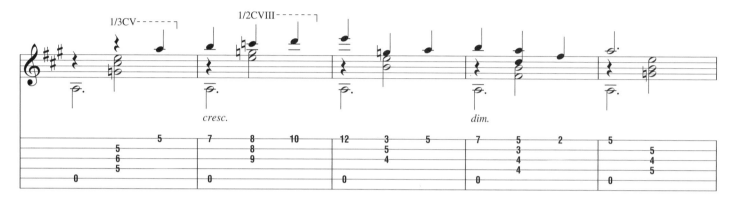

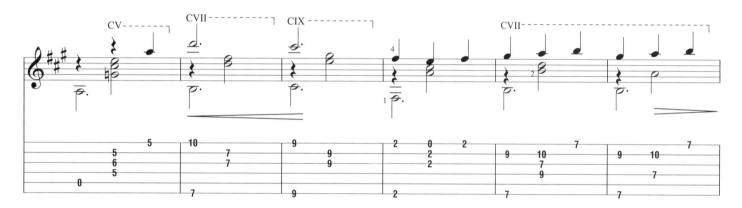

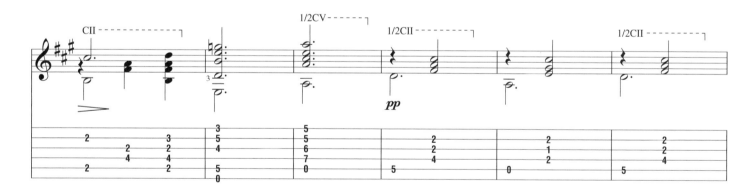

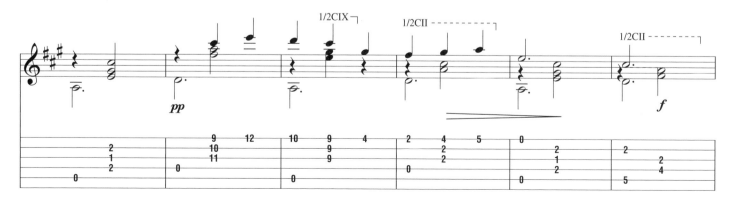

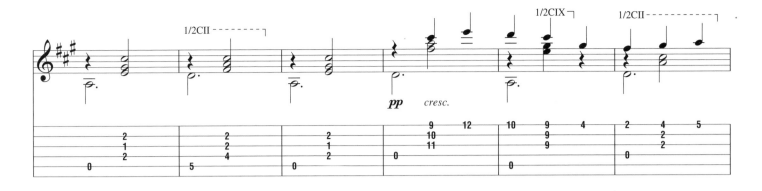

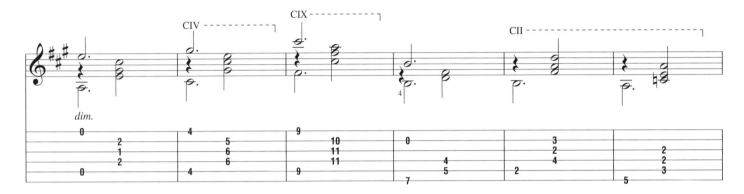

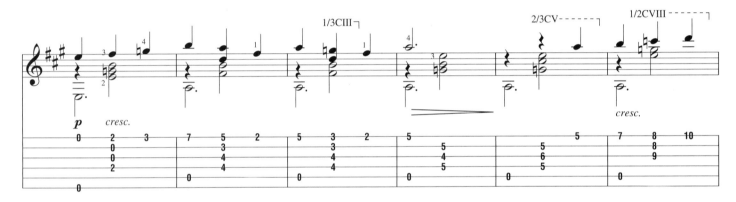

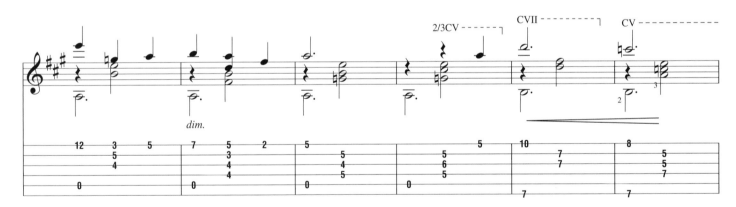

Jesu, Joy of Man's Desiring

Johann Sebastian Bach

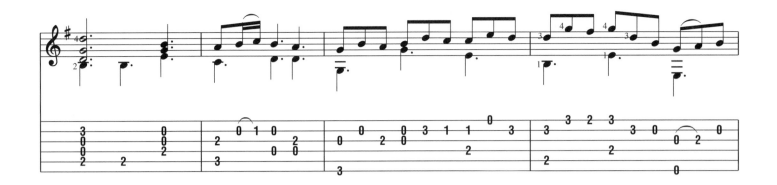

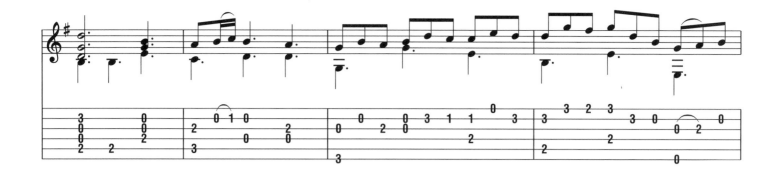

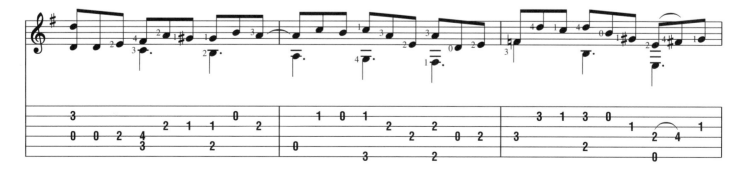

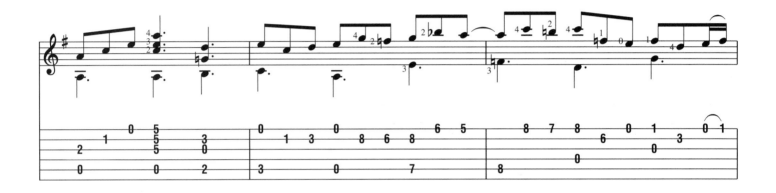

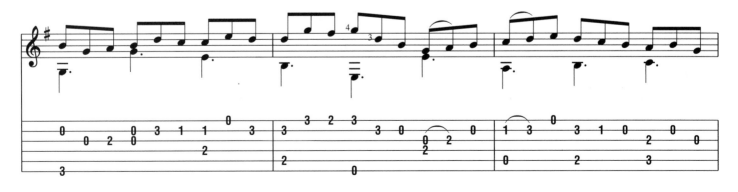

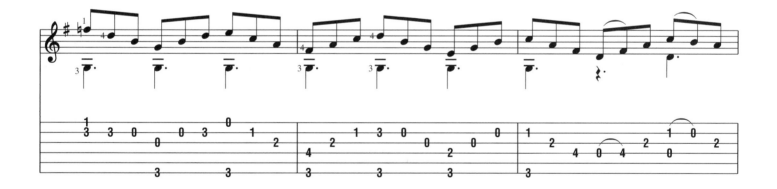

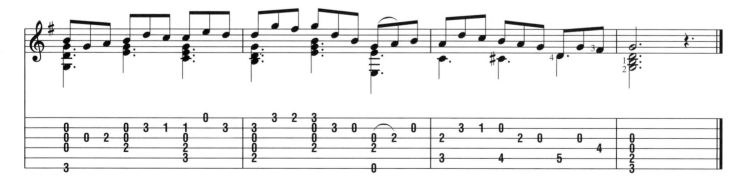

Kemp's Jig

Anonymous 16th Century

Tuning:
(low to high) D-A-D-G-B-E

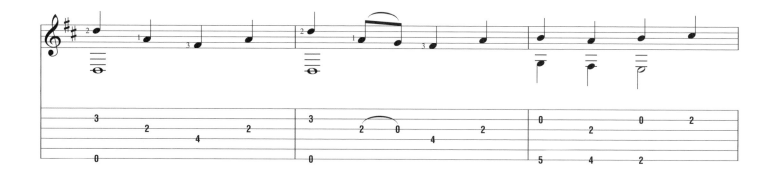

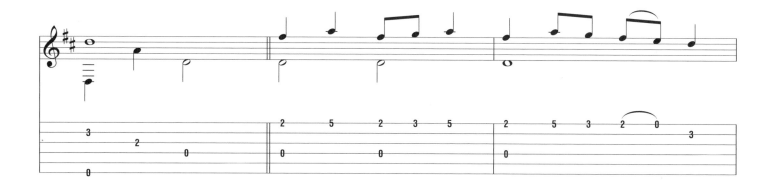

La Volta

from *The Margaret Board Lute Book* (ca.1620-1635)

Tuning:
(low to high) D-A-D-G-B-E

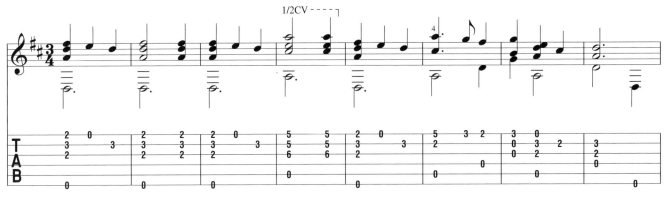

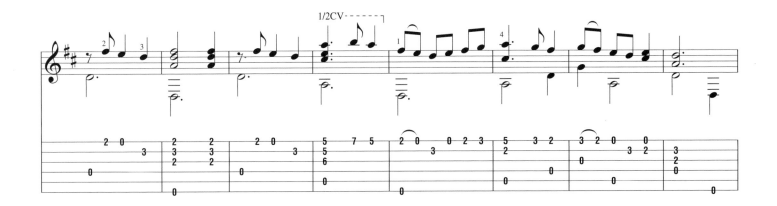

Lord Willoughby's Welcome Home

John Dowland

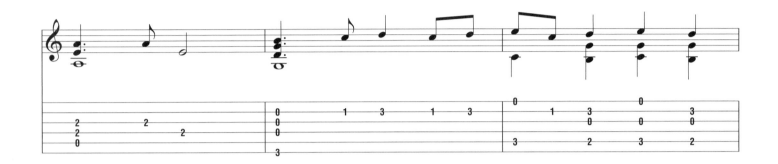

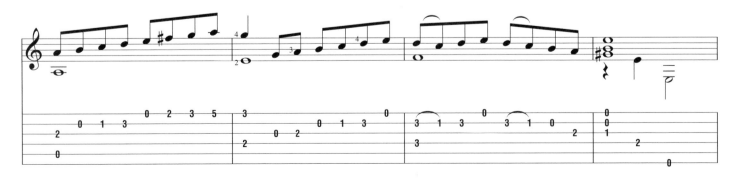

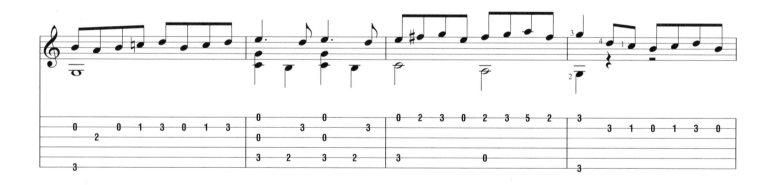

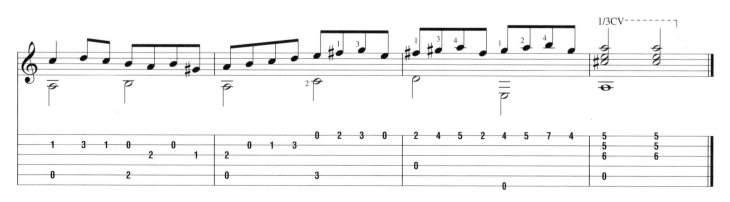

Lágrima

Francisco Tárrega

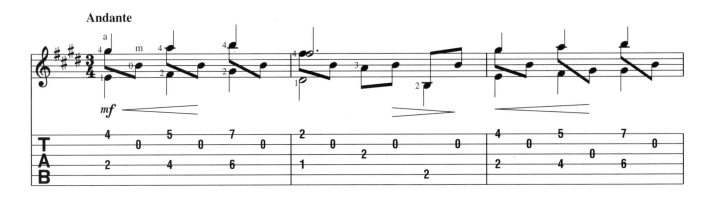

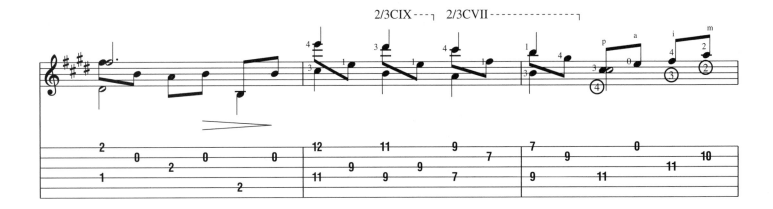

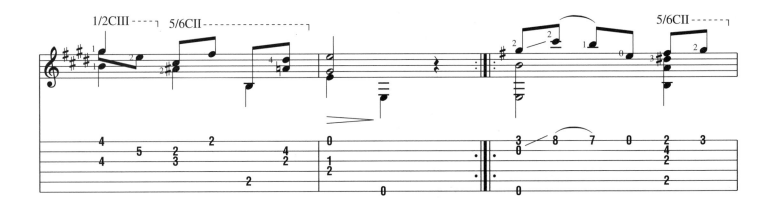

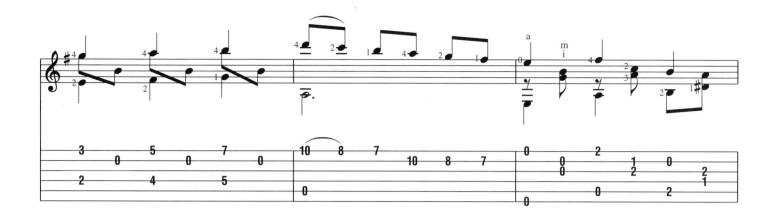

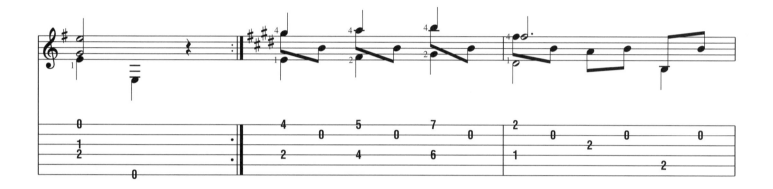

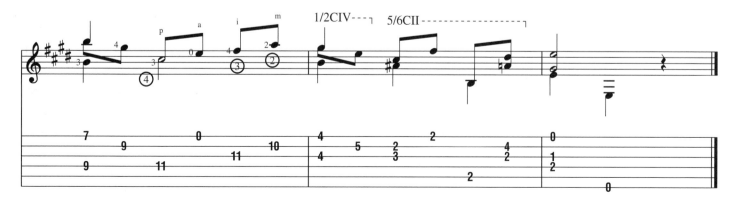

Las Folias de España

Gaspar Sanz

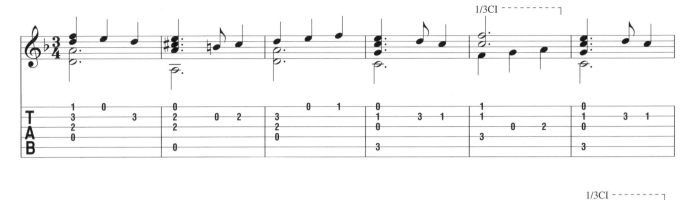

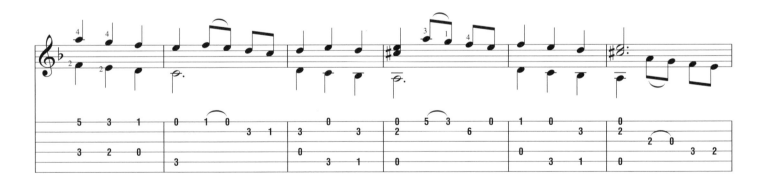

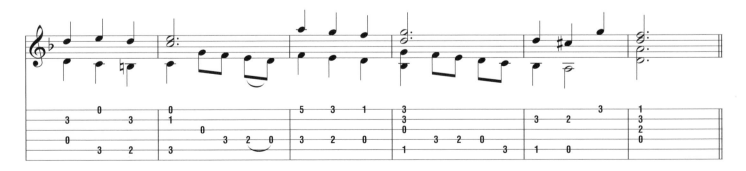

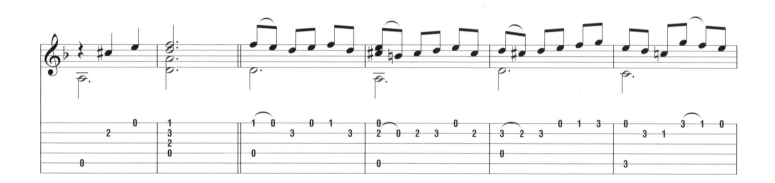

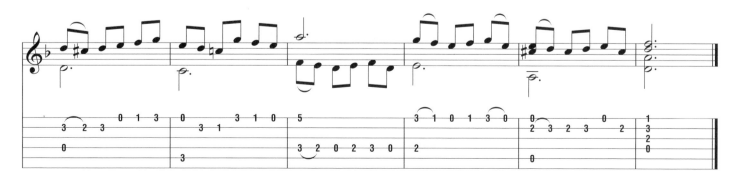

Menuetto

Fernando Sor

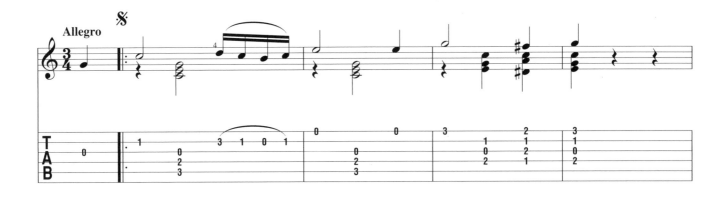

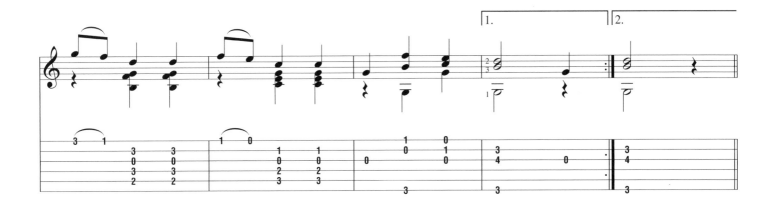

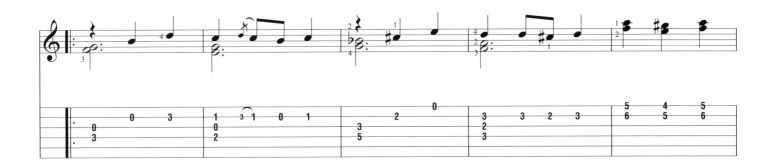

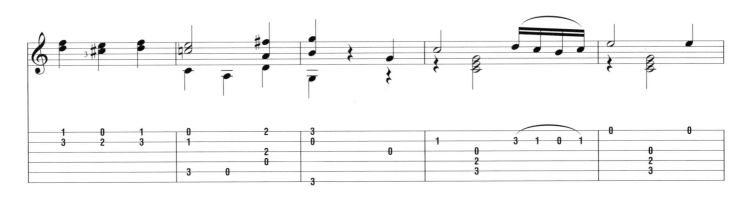

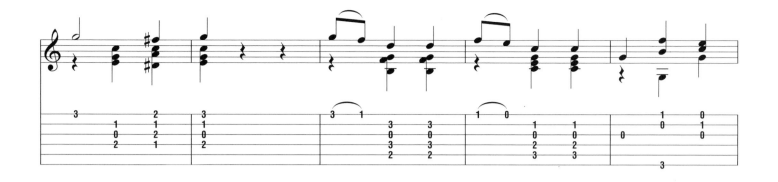

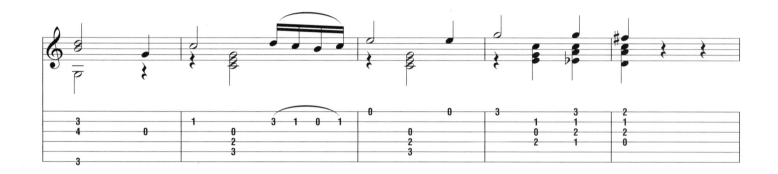

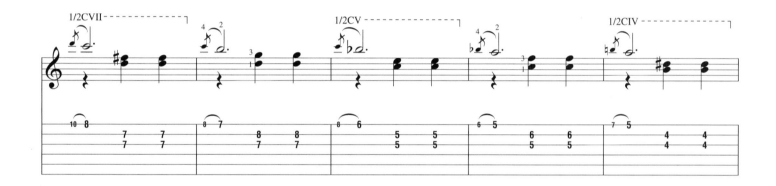

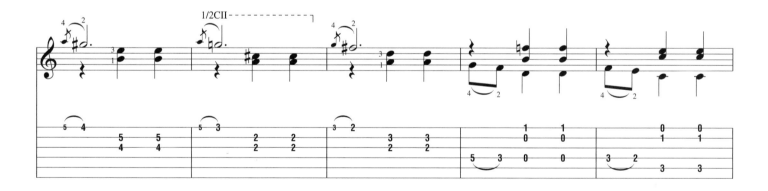

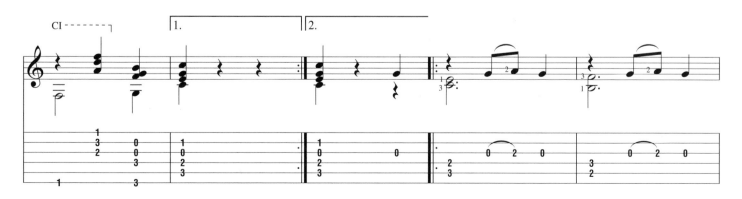

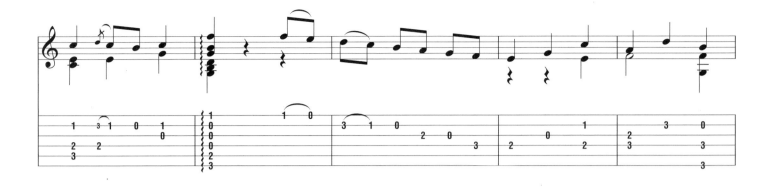

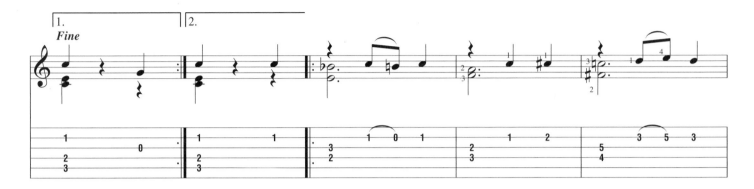

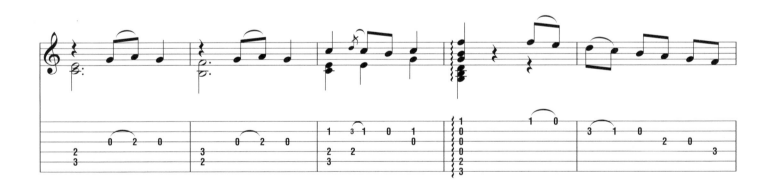

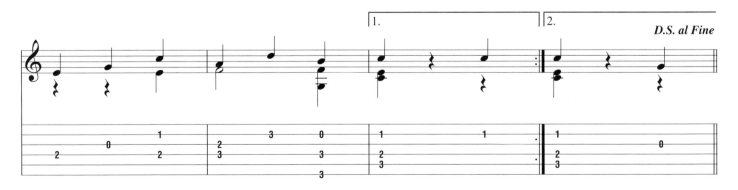

Menuetto

from *Sonata Op. 22*

Fernando Sor

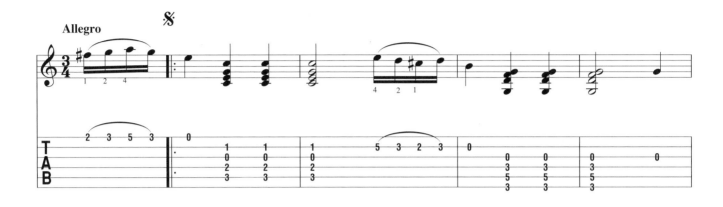

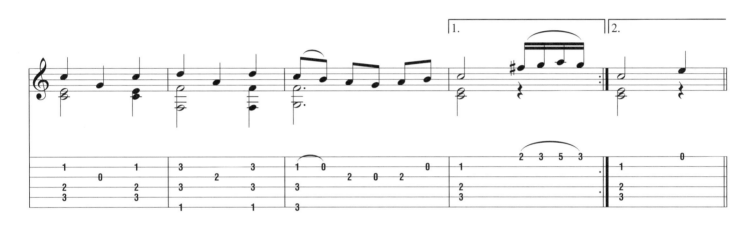

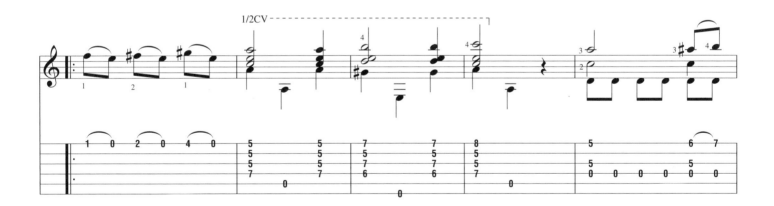

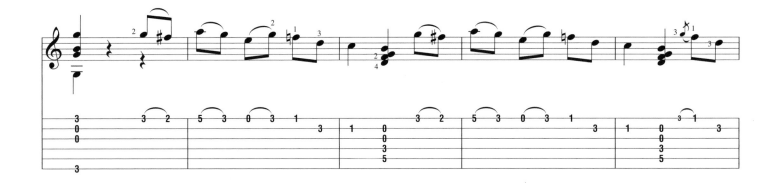

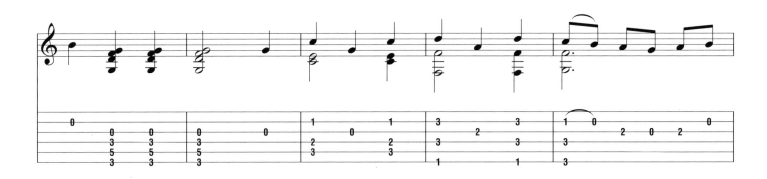

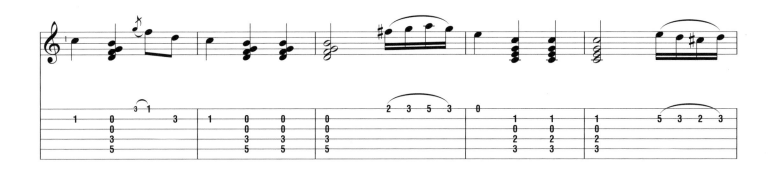

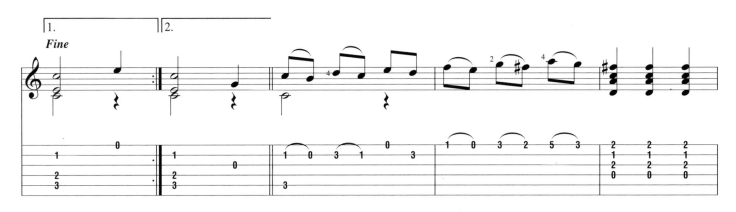

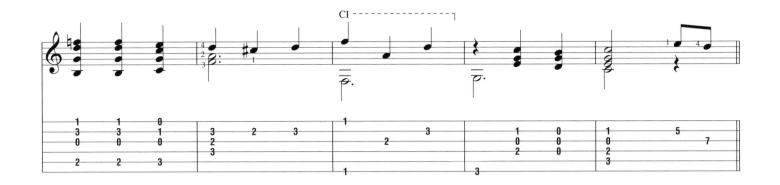

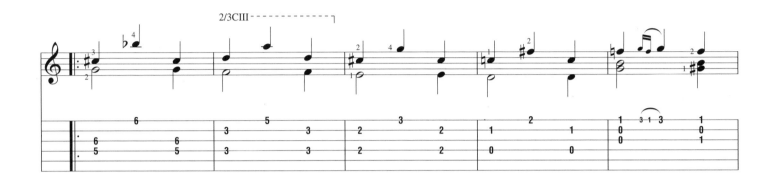

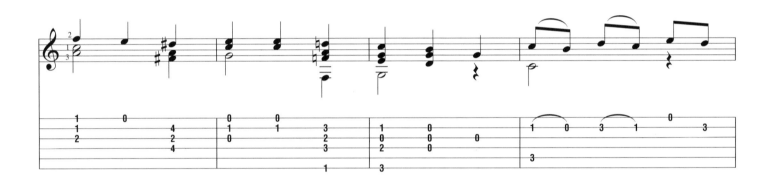

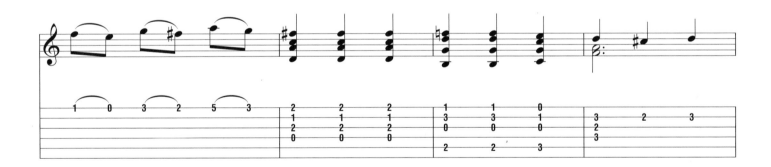

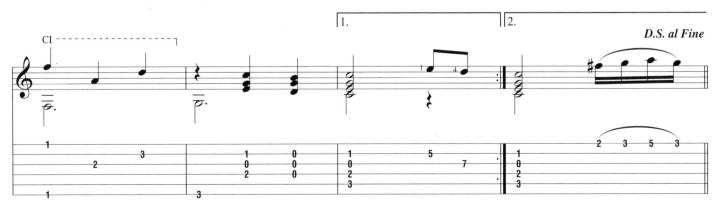

Minuet

Robert de Visee

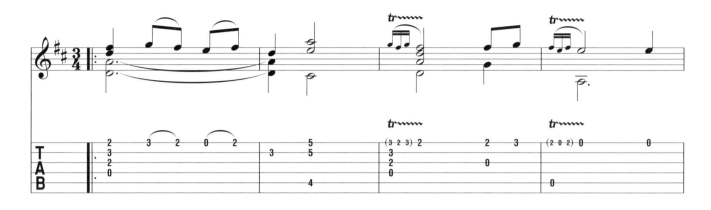

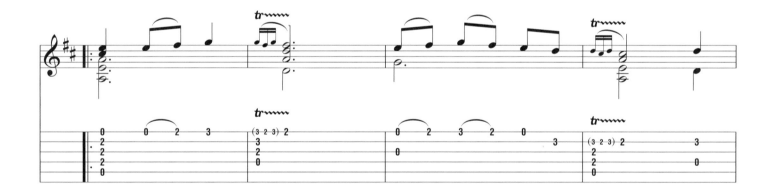

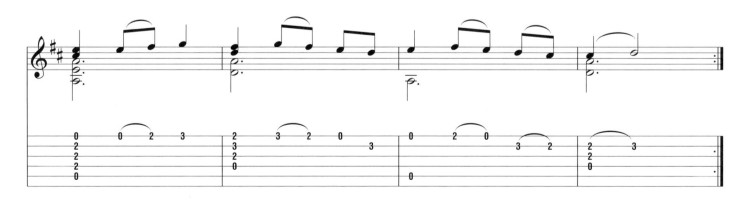

Minuet in G

Johann Sebastian Bach

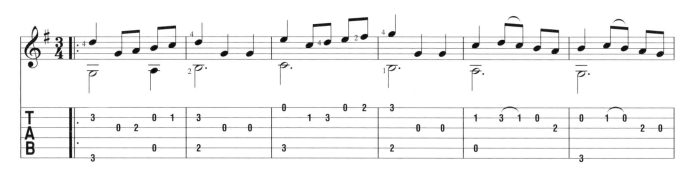

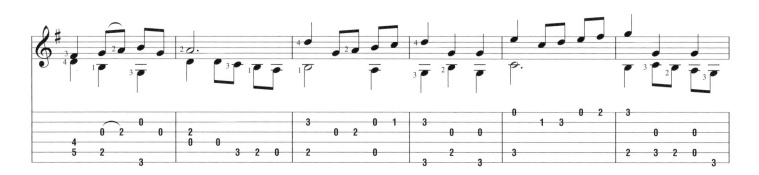

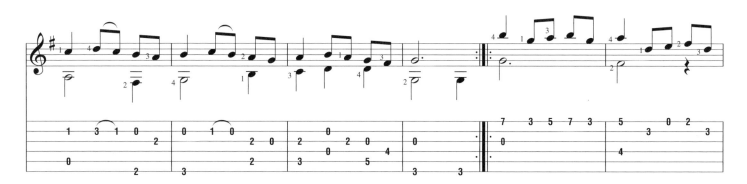

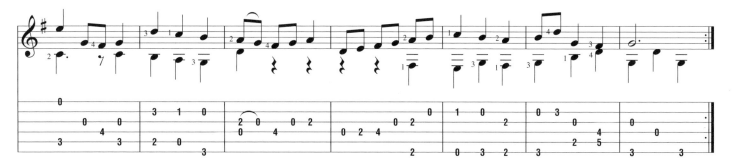

Mistress Winter's Jump

John Dowland

Mrs. Nichols' Almain

John Dowland

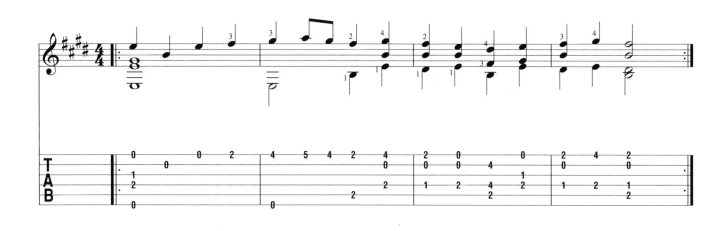

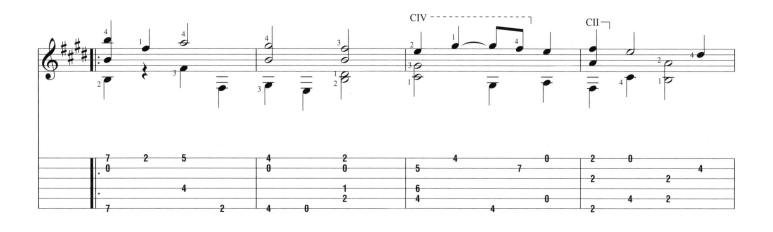

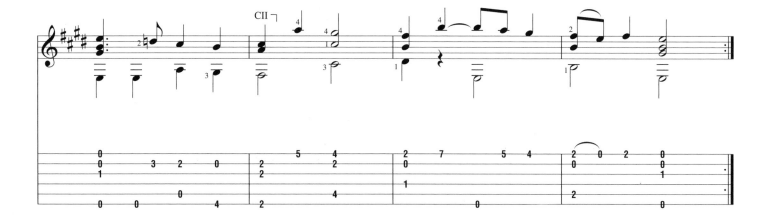

Packington's Pound

Anonymous 16th Century English

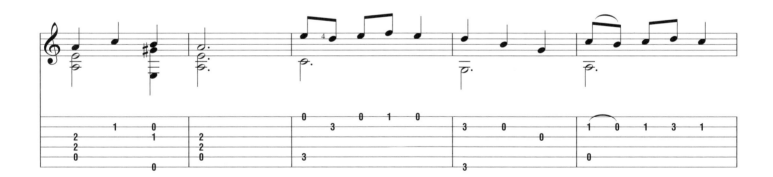

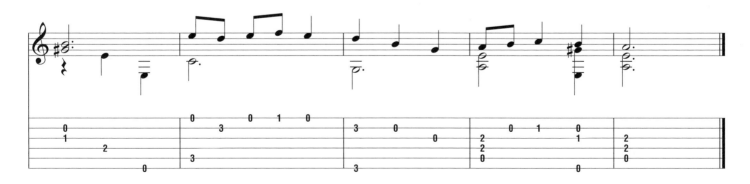

Pavana

Gaspar Sanz

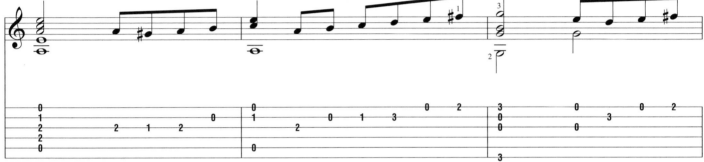

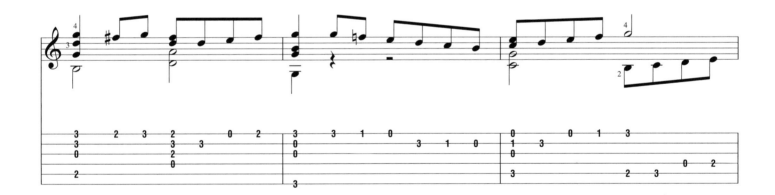

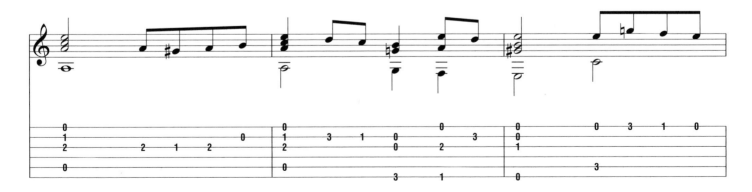

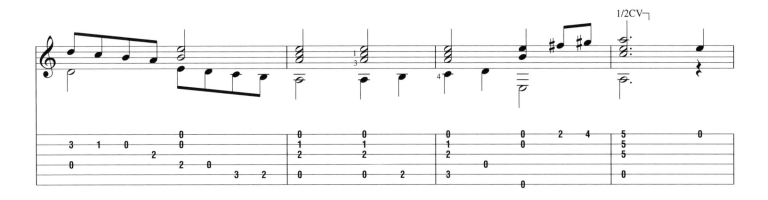

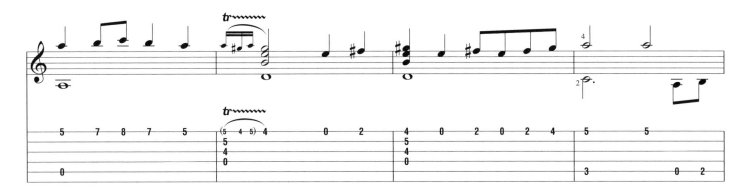

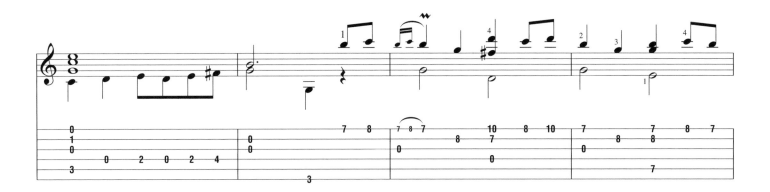

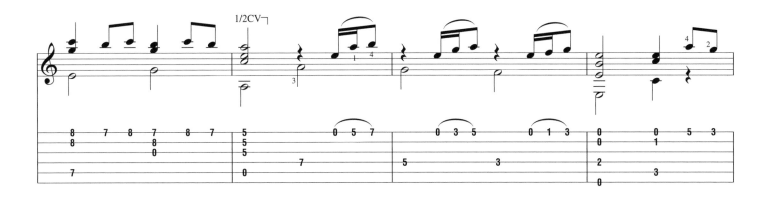

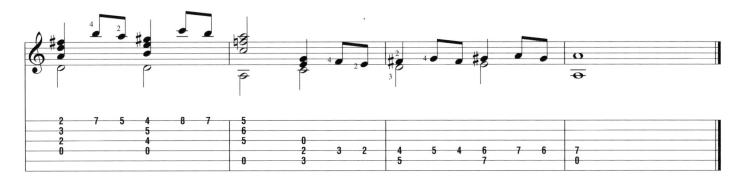

Prelude

Johann Anton Logy

Prelude

Robert de Visee

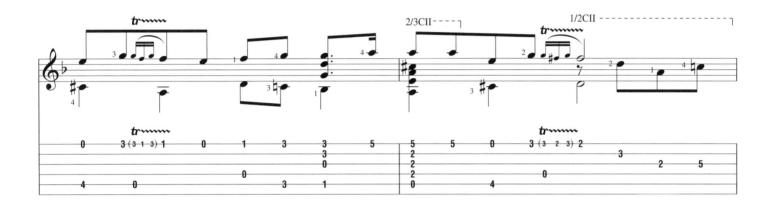

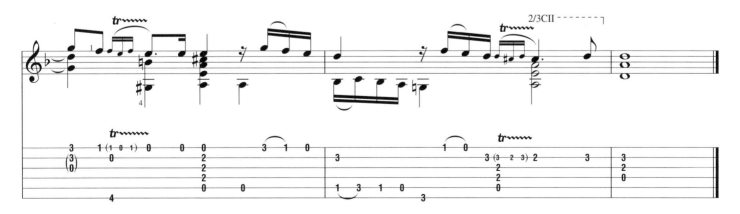

Prelude and Allegro

Santiago de Murcia

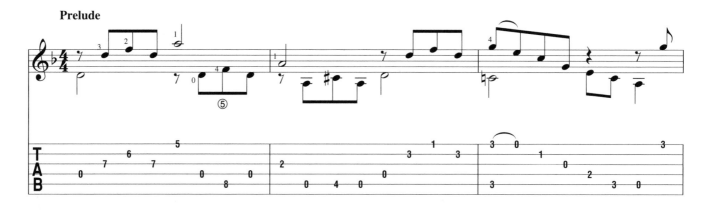

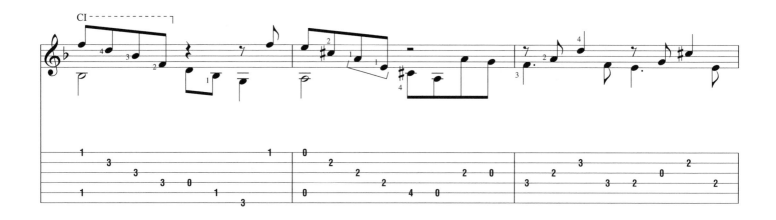

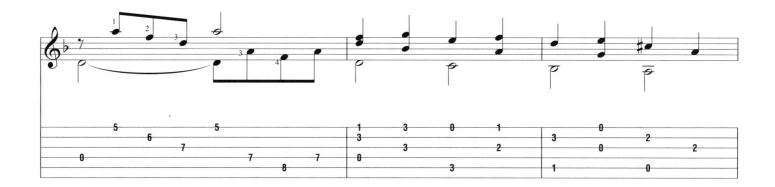

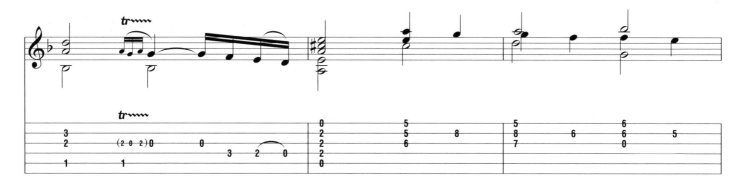

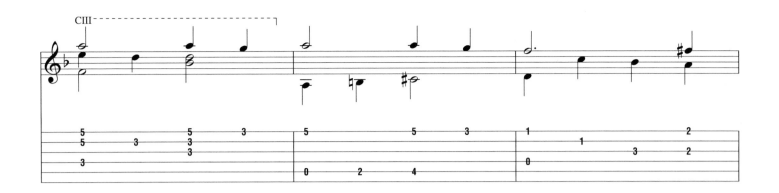

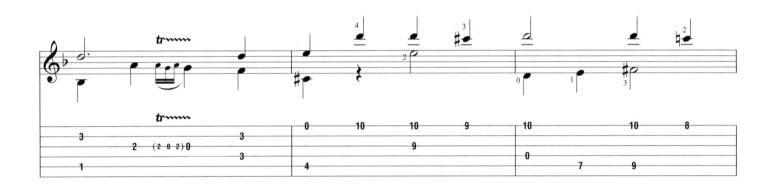

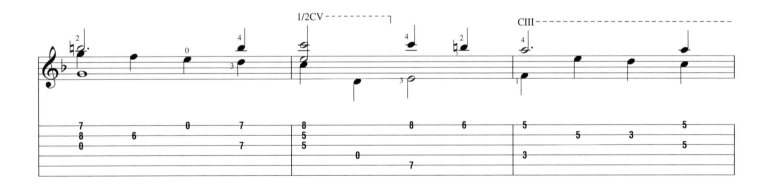

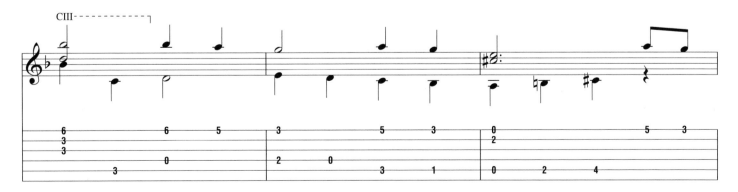

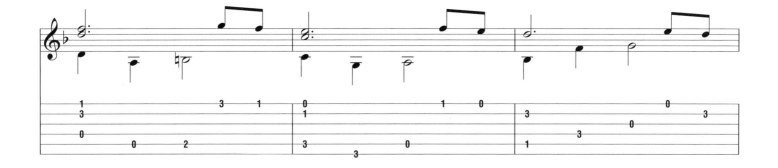

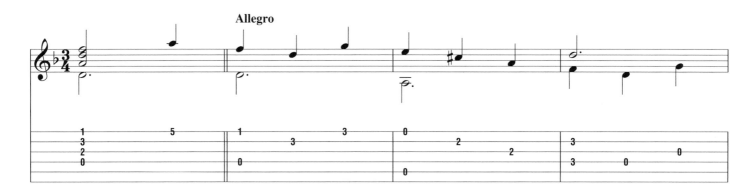

Allegro

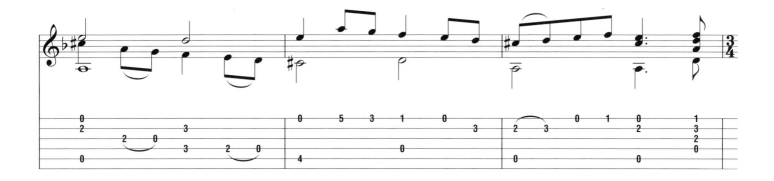

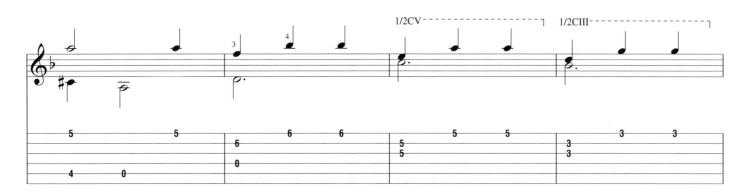

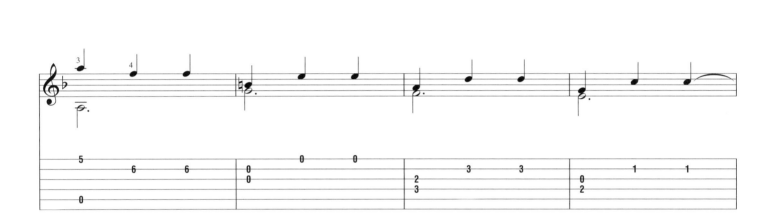

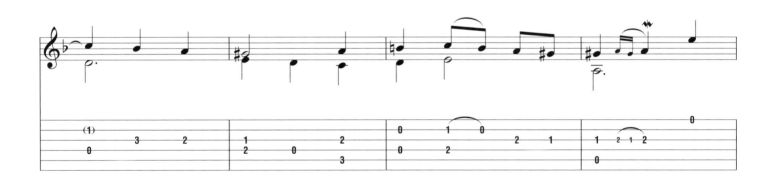

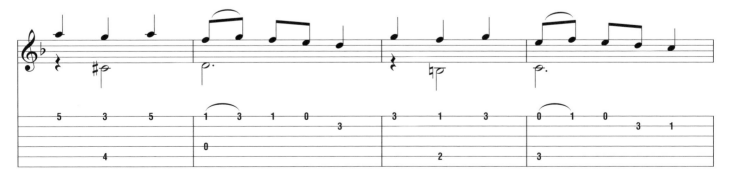

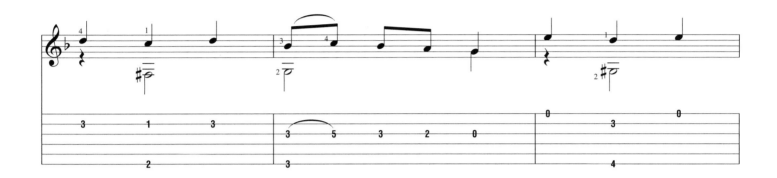

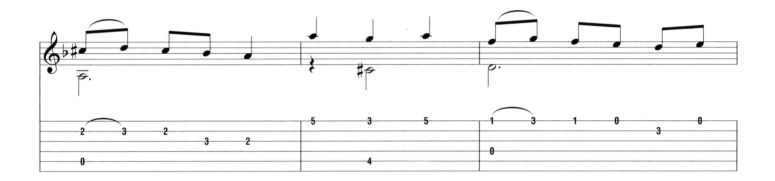

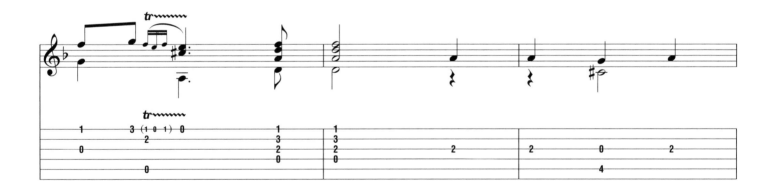

Sarabande

Johann Anton Logy

Recuerdos de la Alhambra

Francisco Tárrega

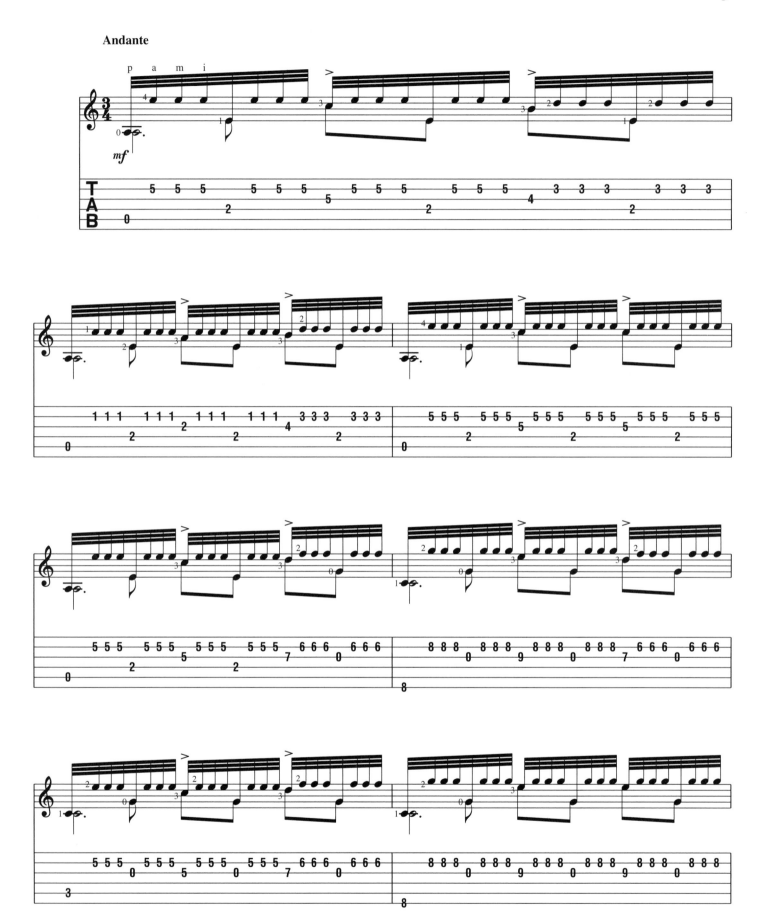

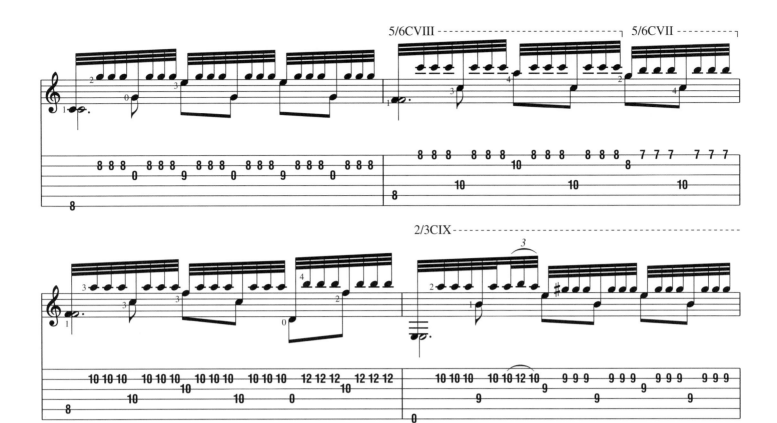

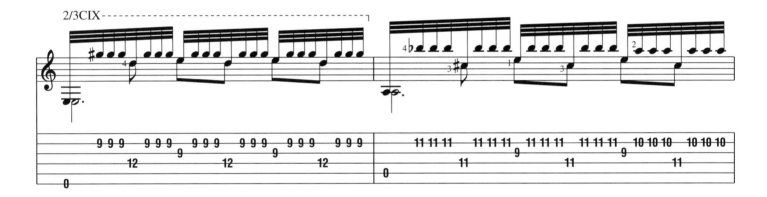

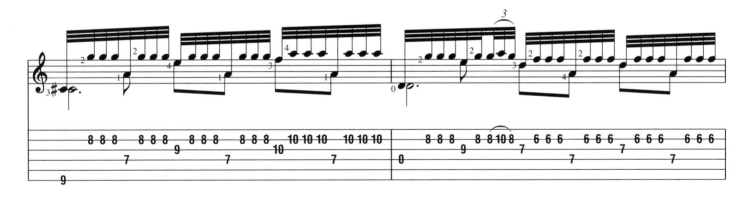

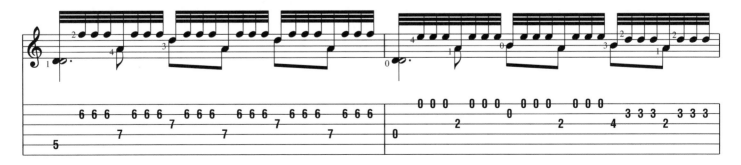

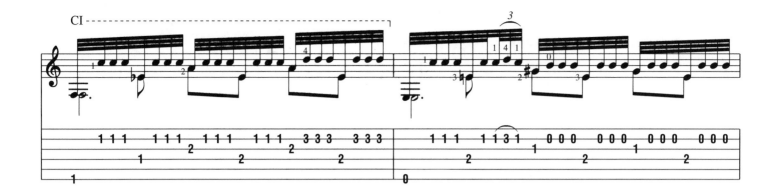

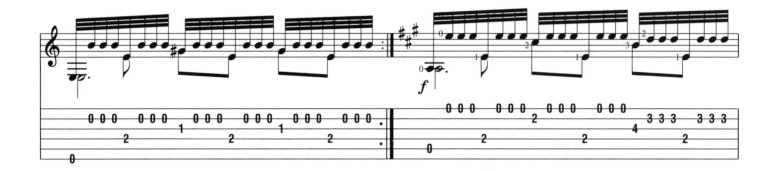

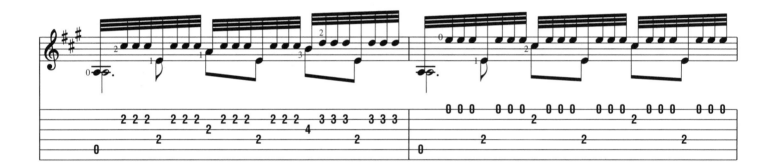

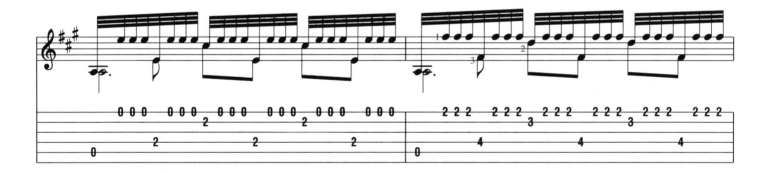

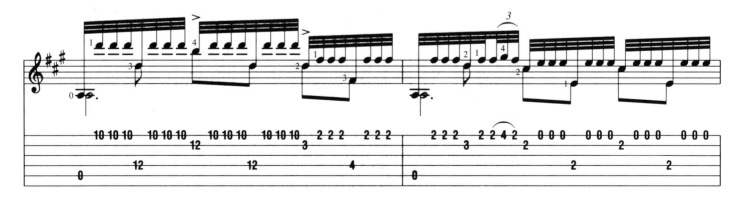

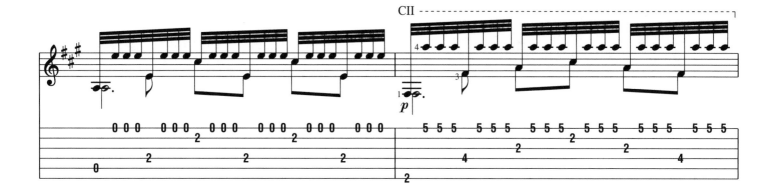

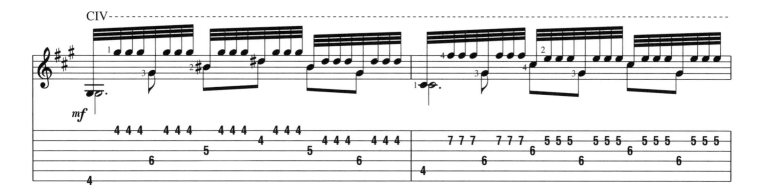

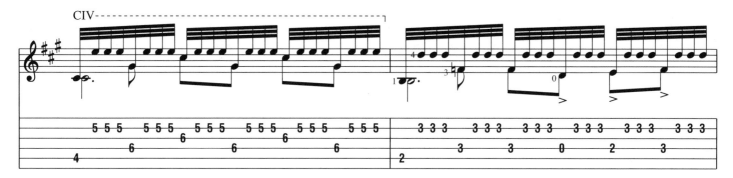

To Coda ⊕

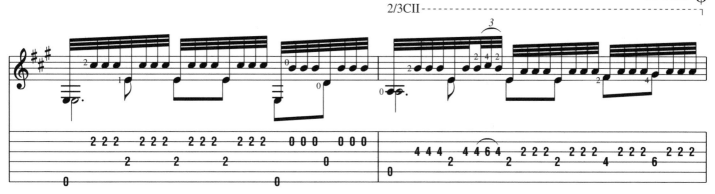

1.

2.

D.C. al Coda
(without repeats)

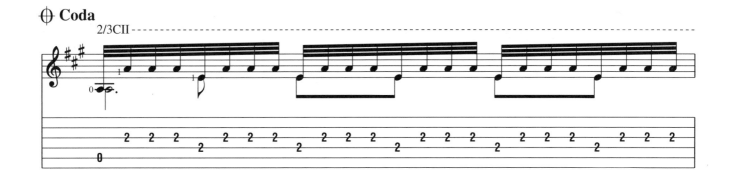

⊕ Coda

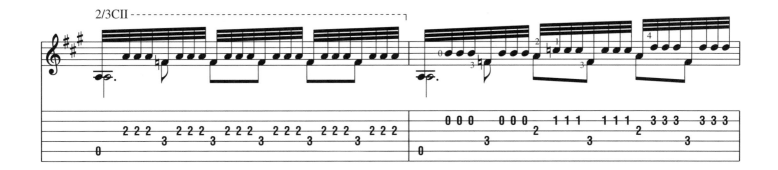

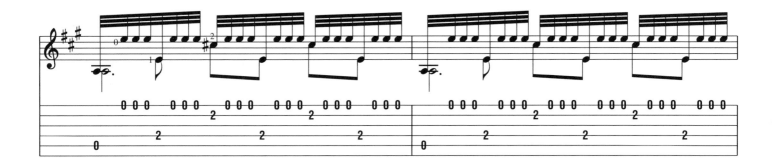

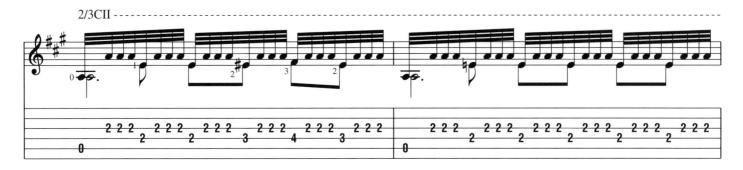

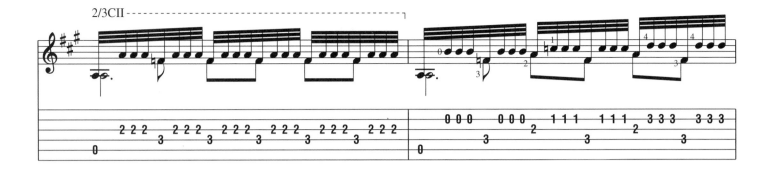

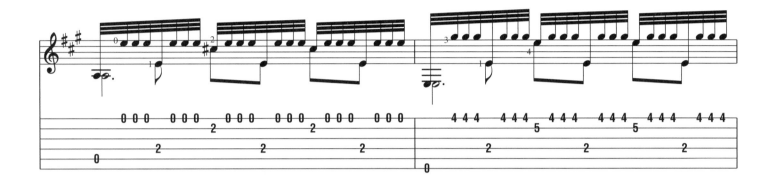

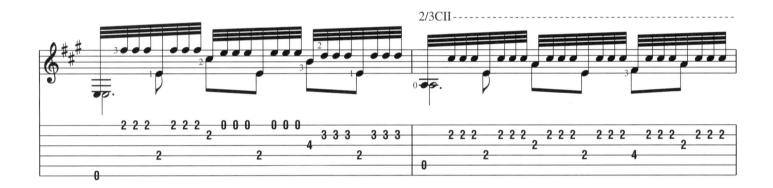

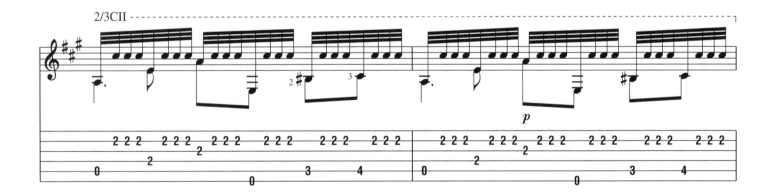

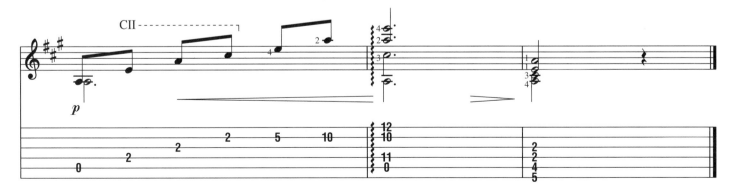

Rondo

Napoleon Coste

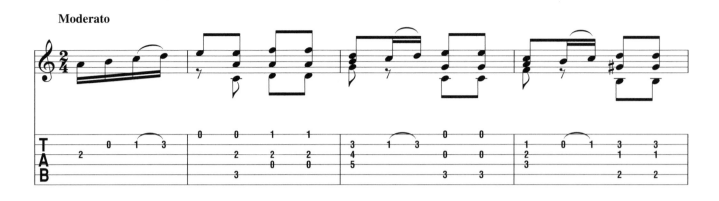

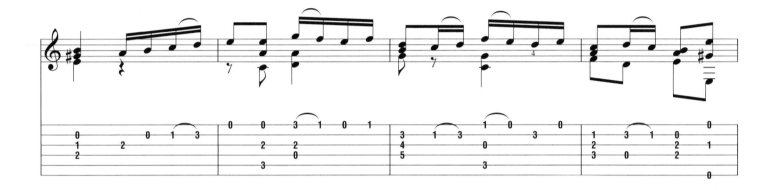

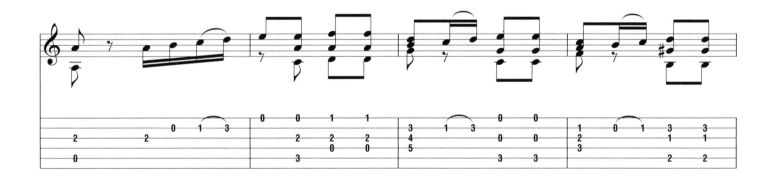

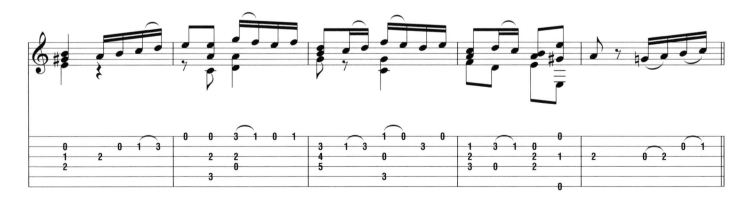

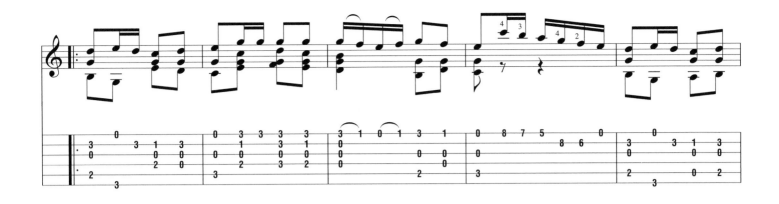

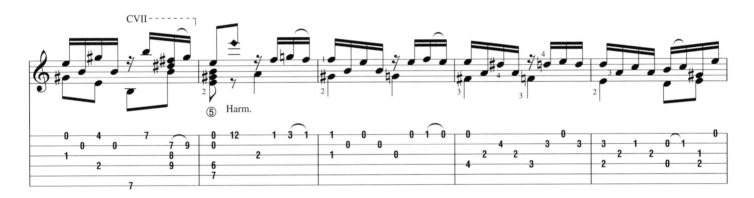

Rujero

Gaspar Sanz

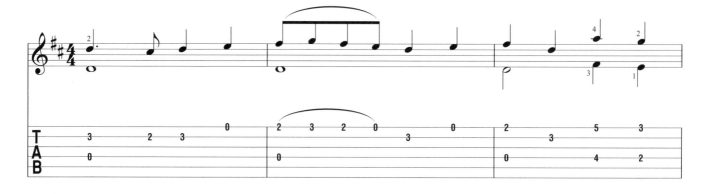

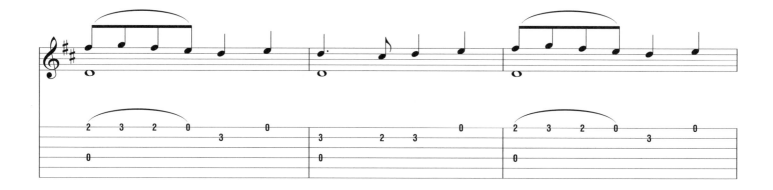

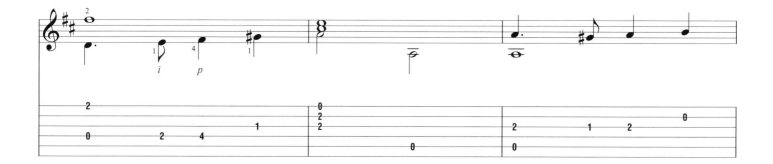

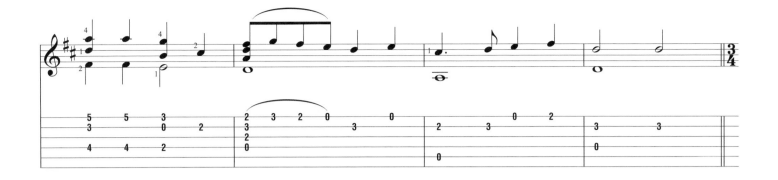

Paradetes

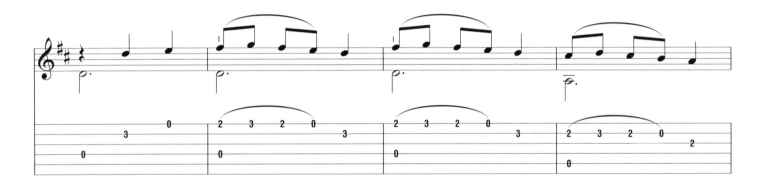

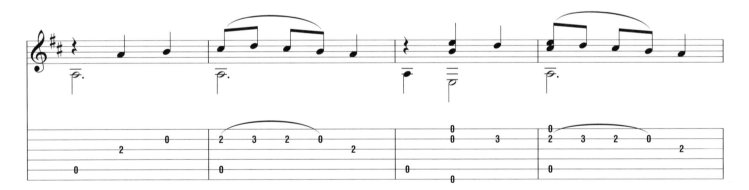

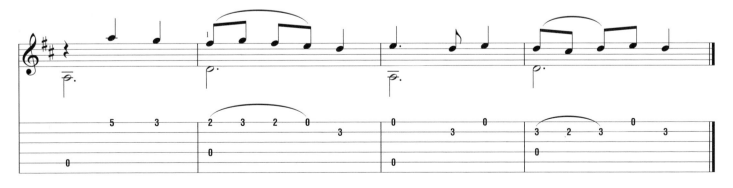

Sarabande

Robert de Visee

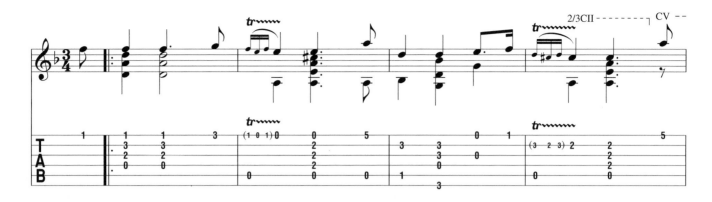

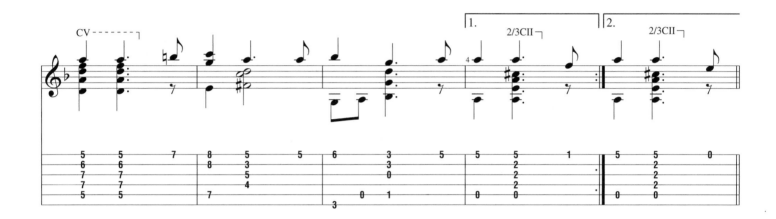

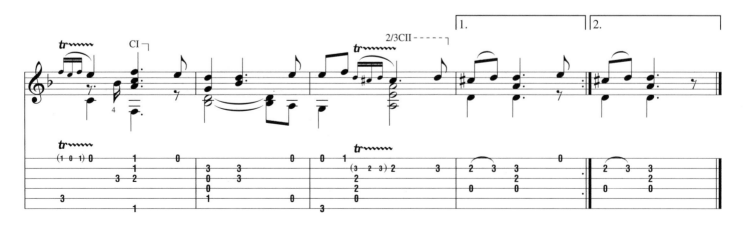

Study in A Minor

Dionisio Aguado

Se io m'accorgo

Anonymous Italian 16th Century

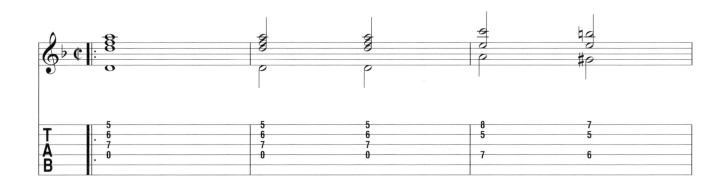

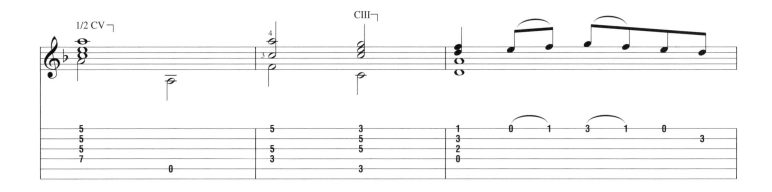

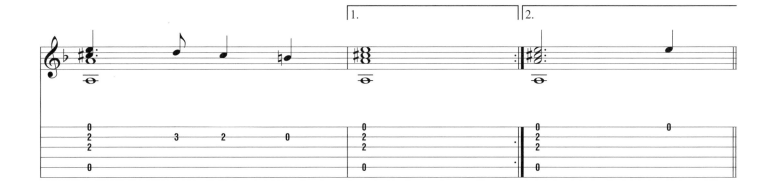

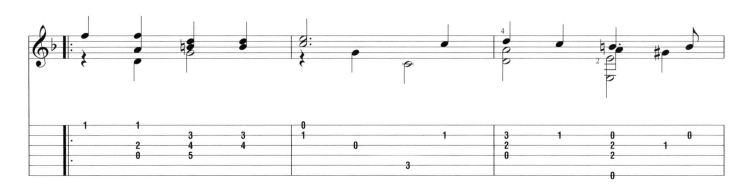

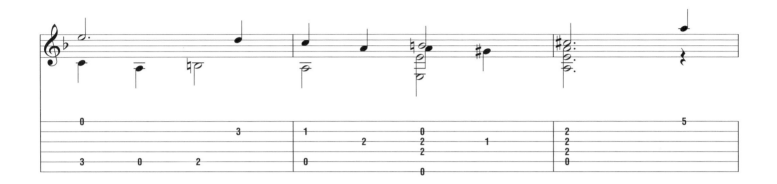

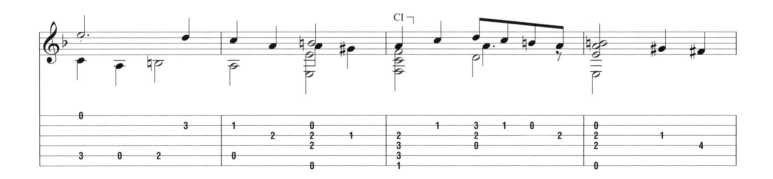

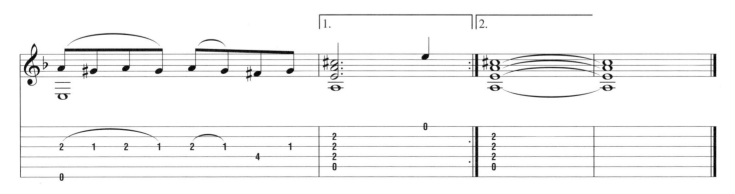

Spanish Romance

Anonymous

Slowly

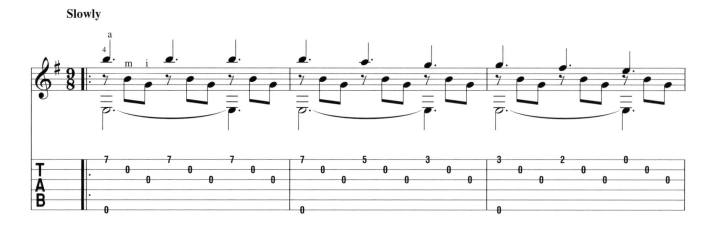

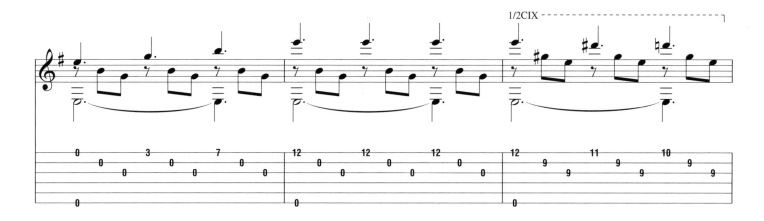

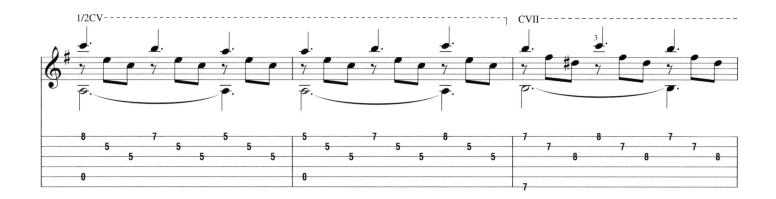

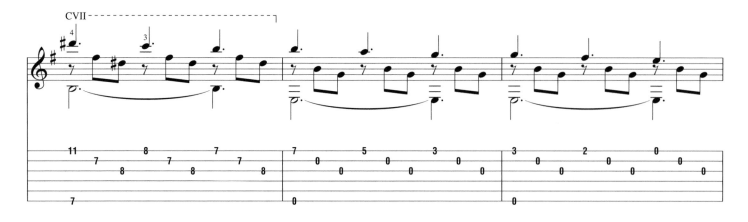

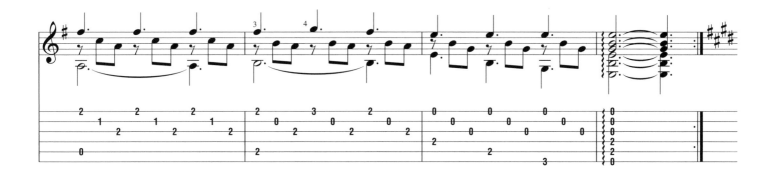

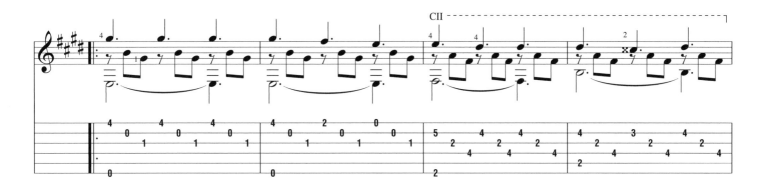

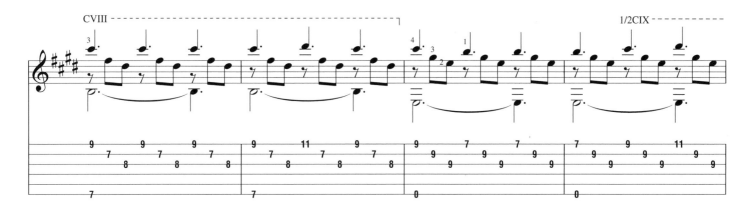

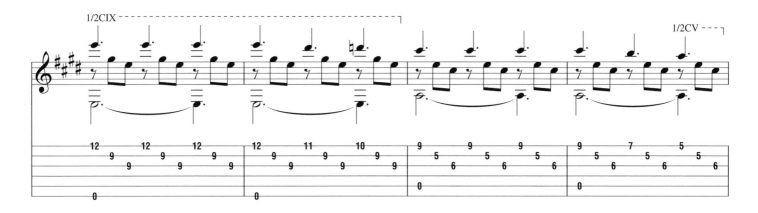

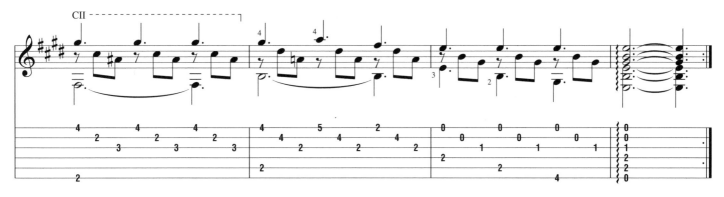

Study No. 2

Fernando Sor

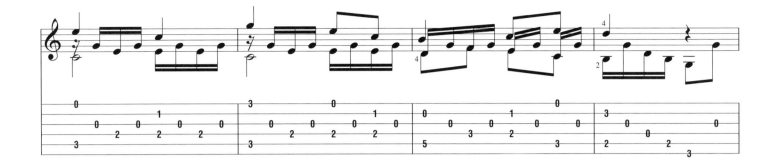

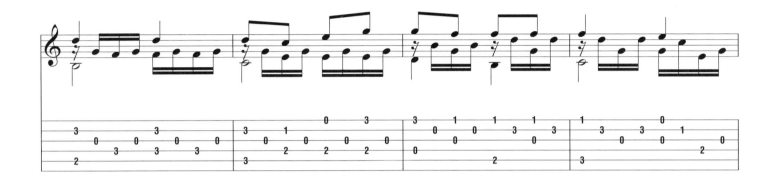

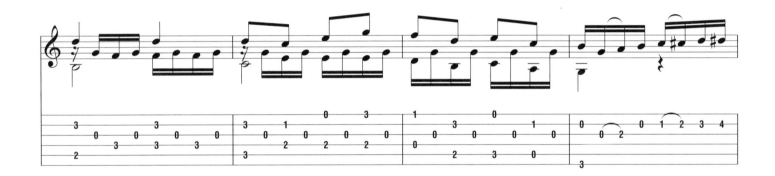

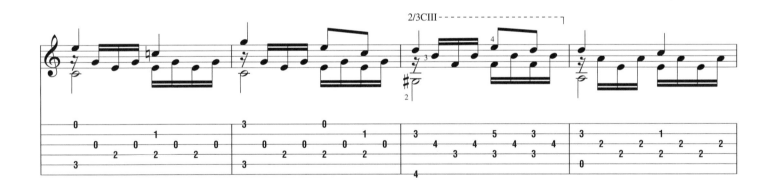

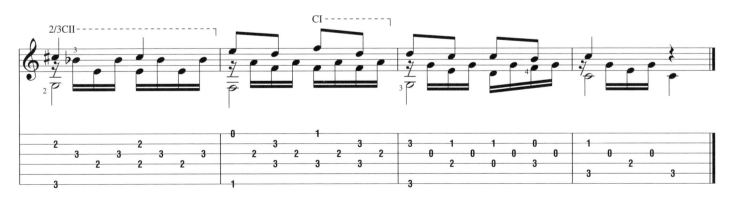

Study No. 5

Fernando Sor

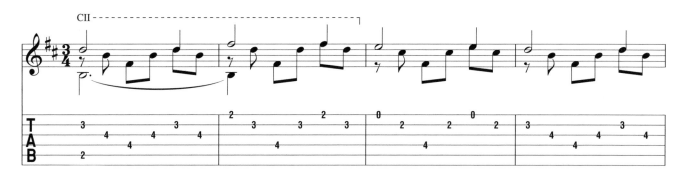

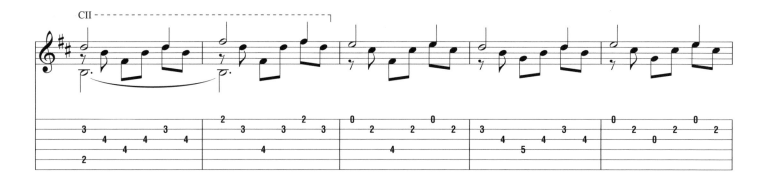

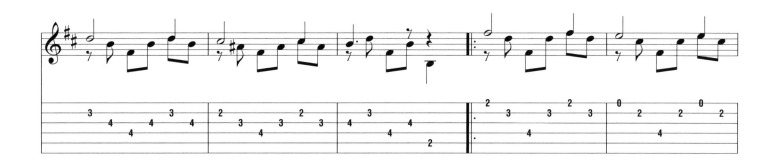

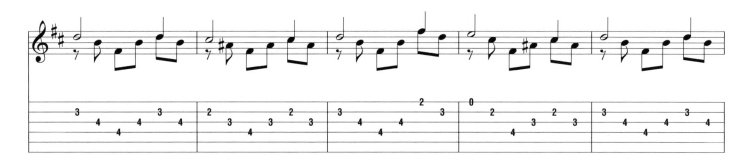

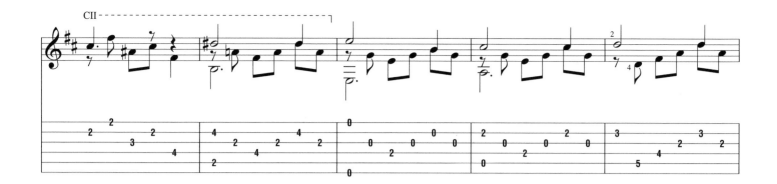

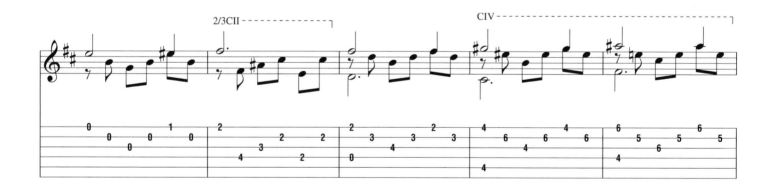

Study No. 6

Fernando Sor

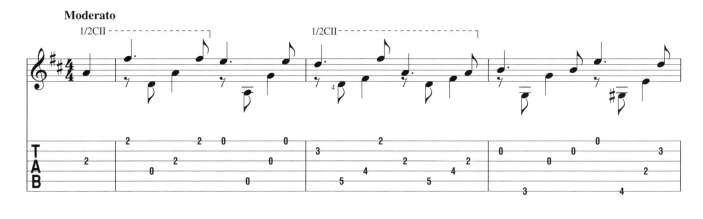

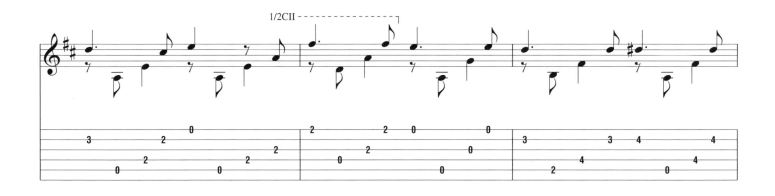

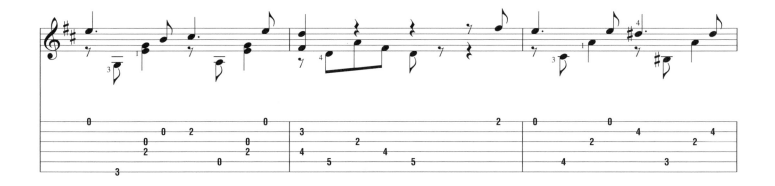

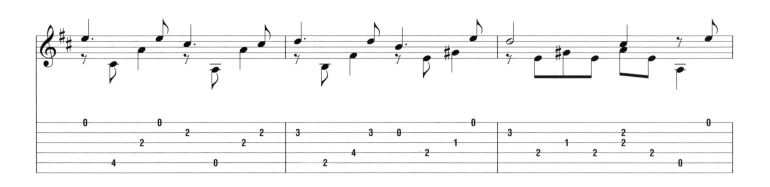

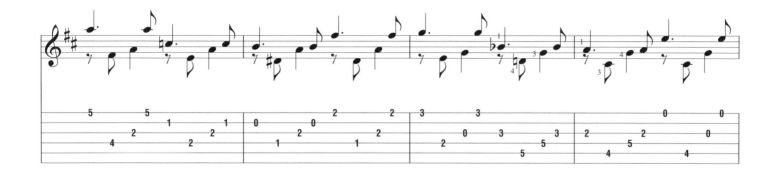

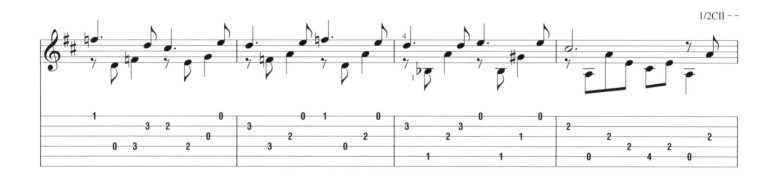

Study
Op. 60, No. 3

Matteo Carcassi

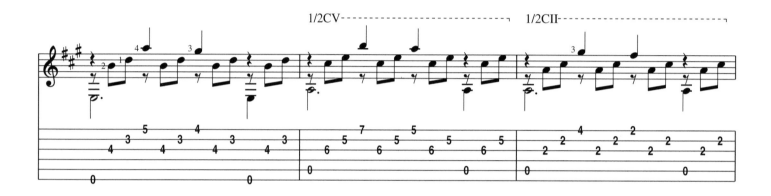

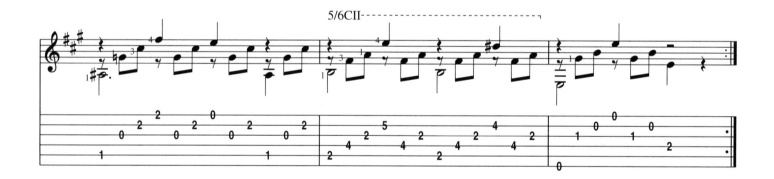

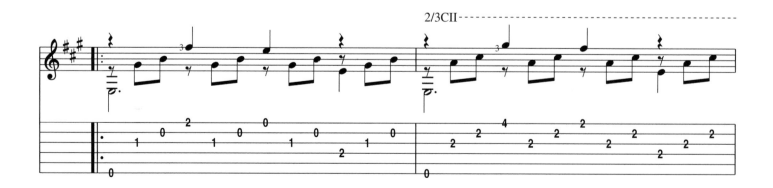

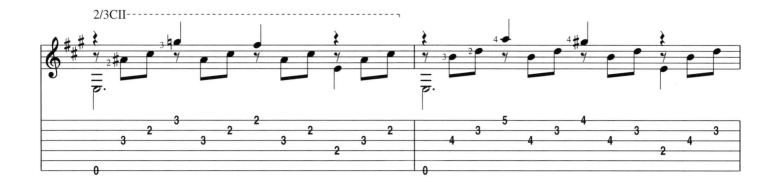

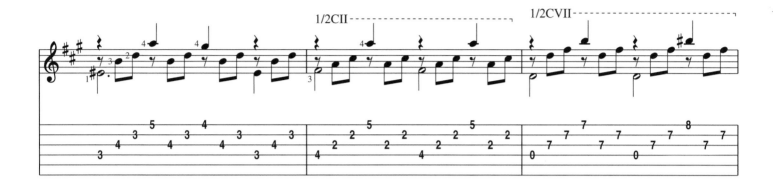

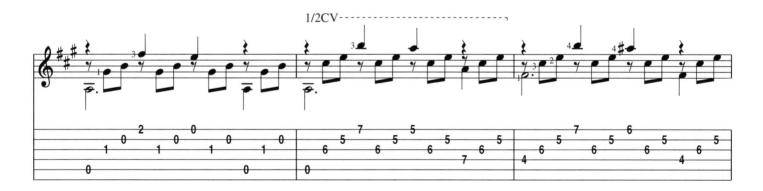

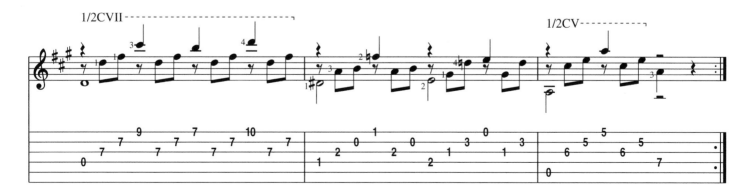

Study
Op. 60, No. 7

Matteo Carcassi

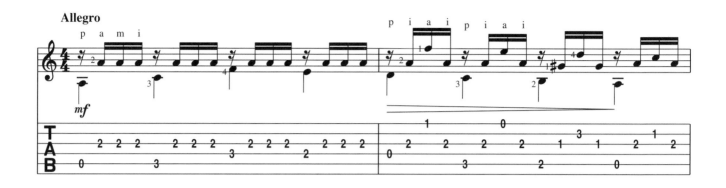

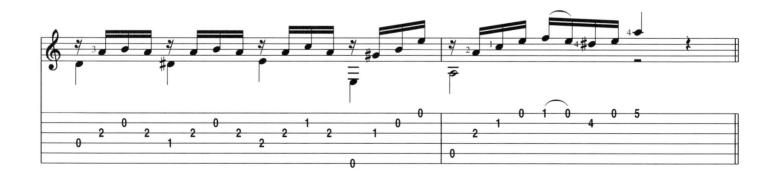

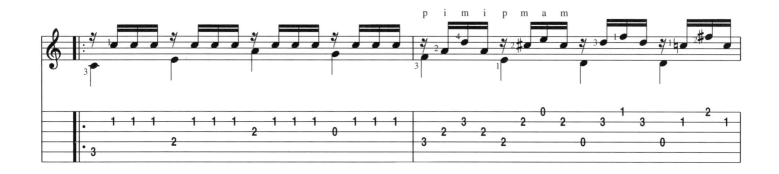

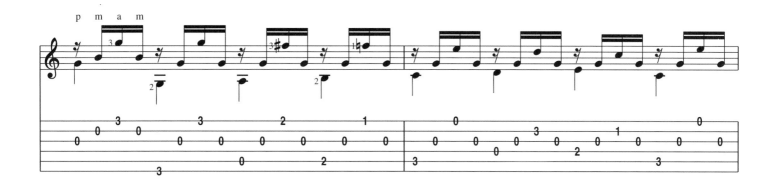

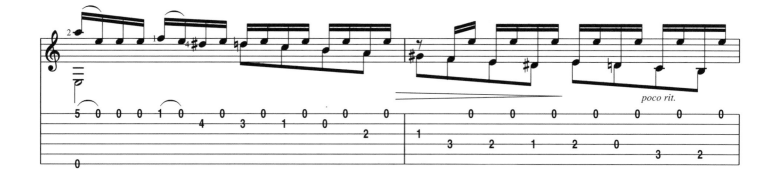

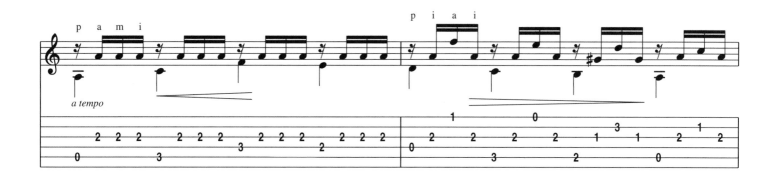

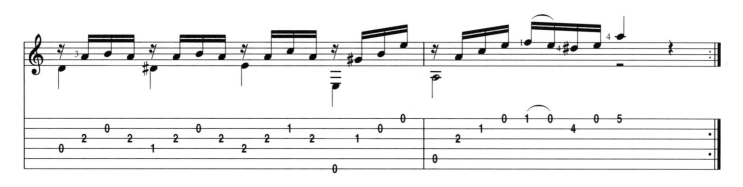

Theme and Variations

Mauro Giuliani

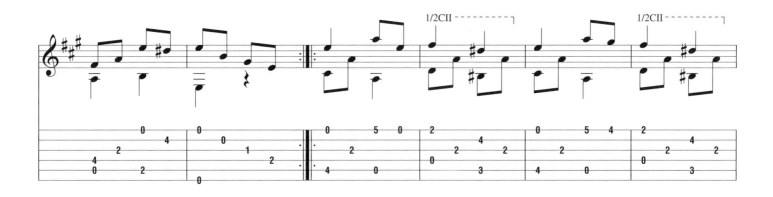

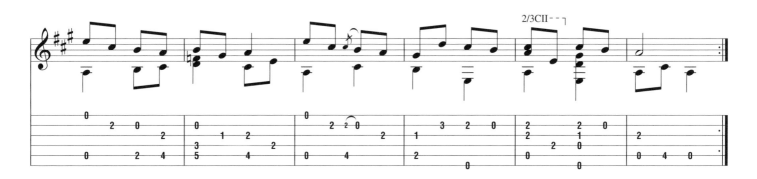

Variation 2

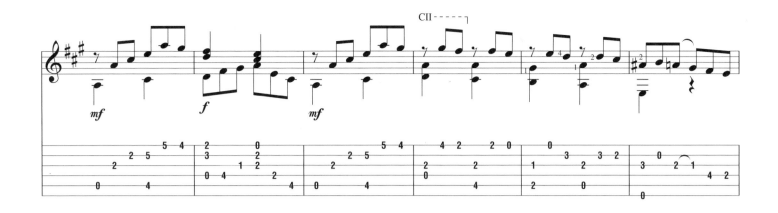

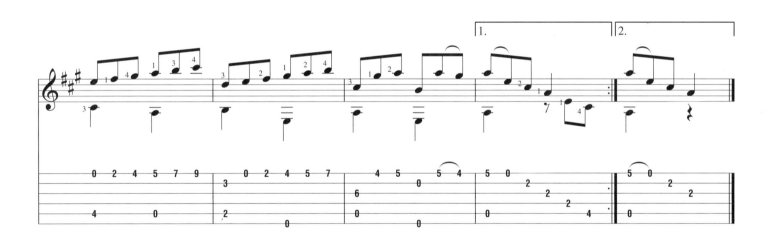

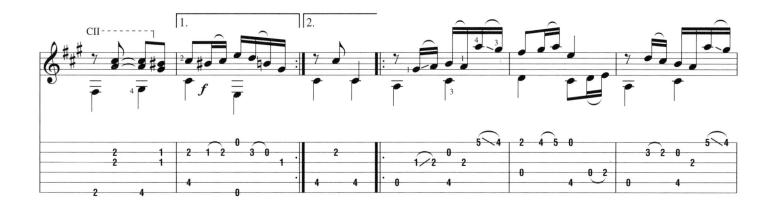

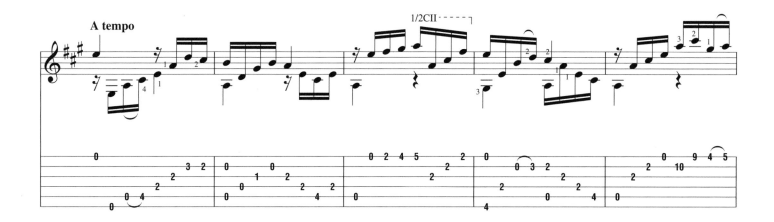

Variation 4

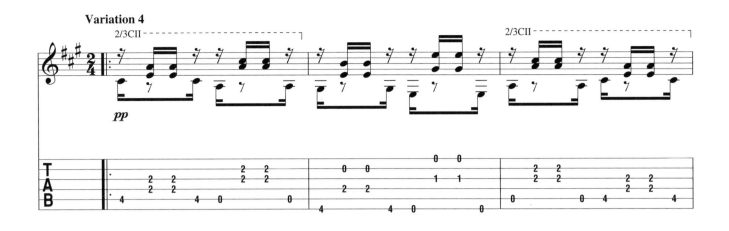

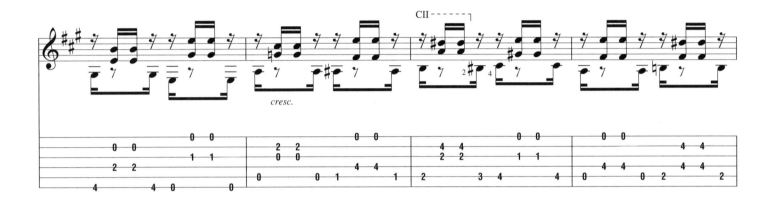

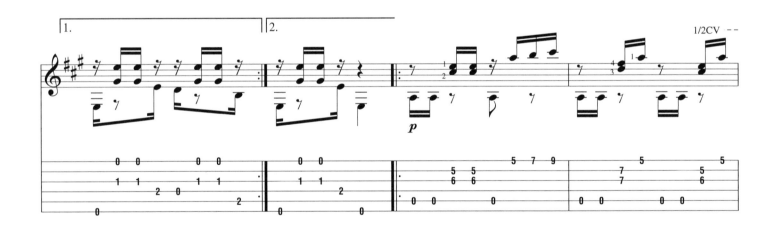

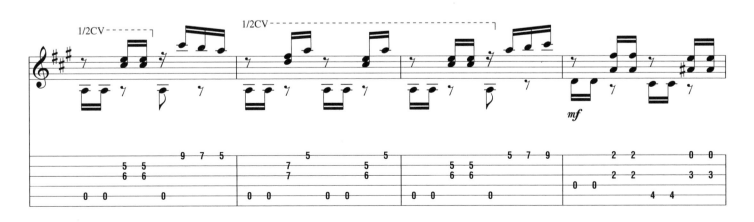

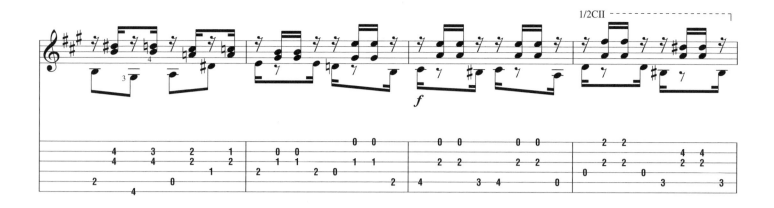

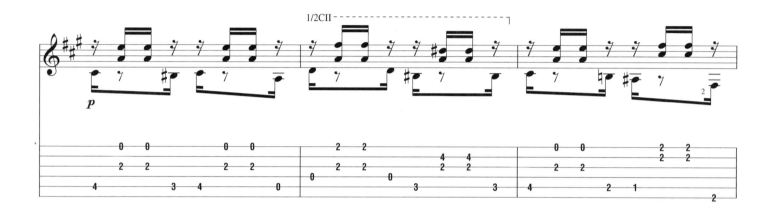

Variation 5
un poco piú Adagio

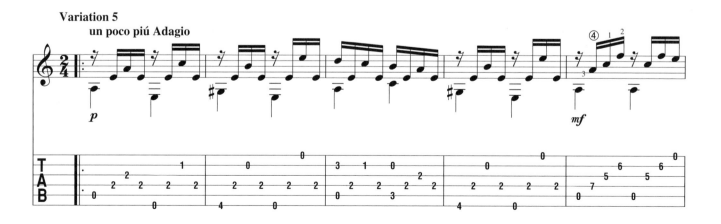

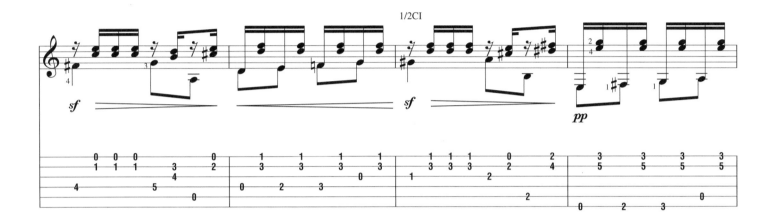

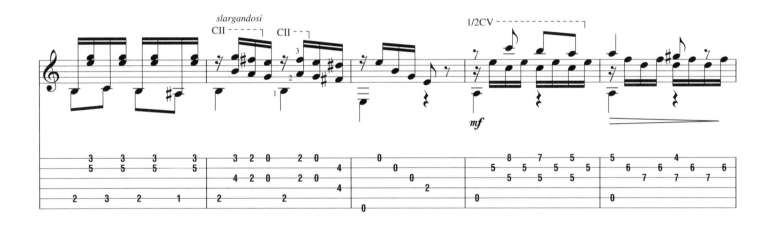

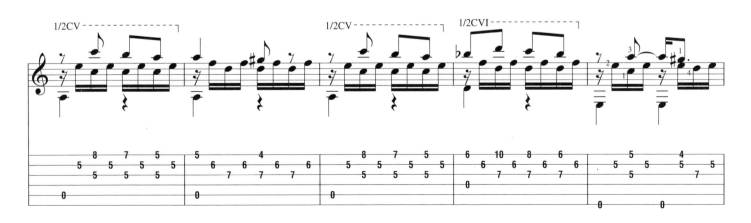

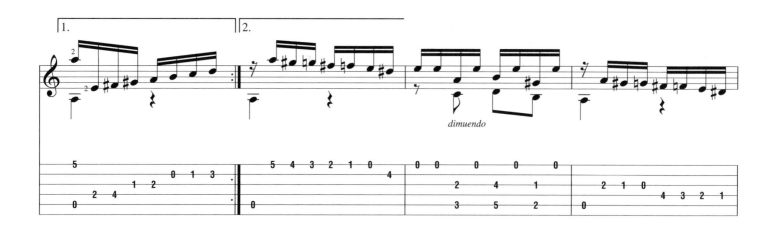

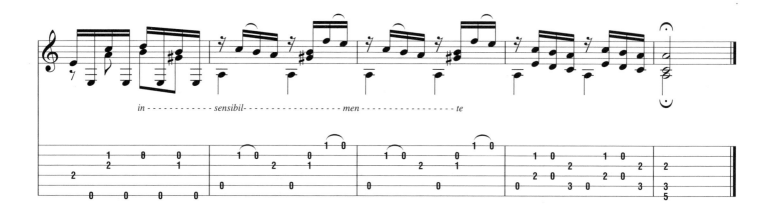

in - - - - - - - - - - - sensibil- - - - - - - - - - - - - men - - - - - - - - - - - - - te

Variation 6

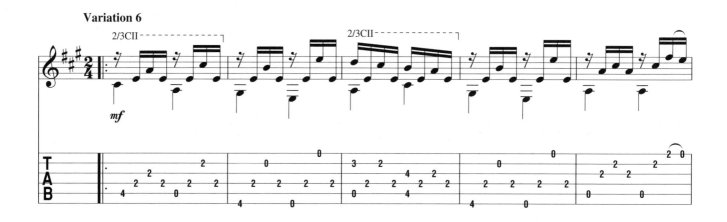

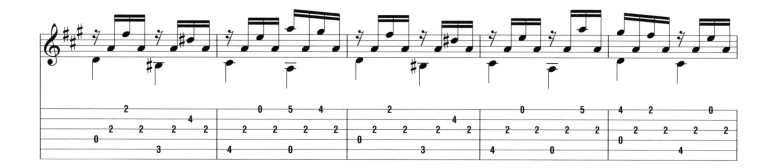

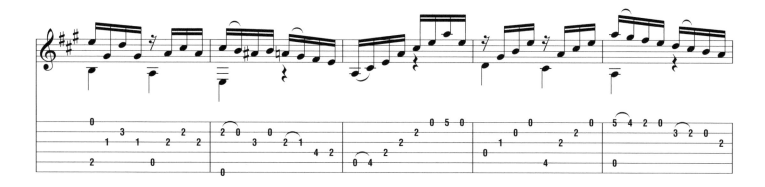

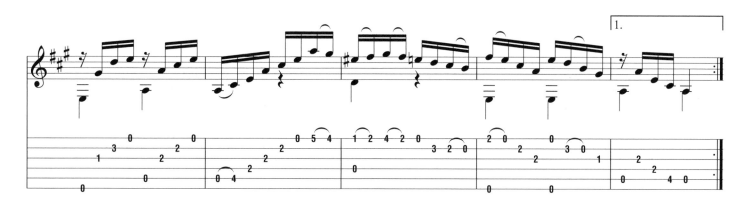

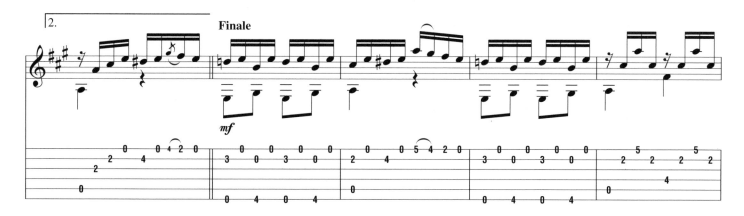

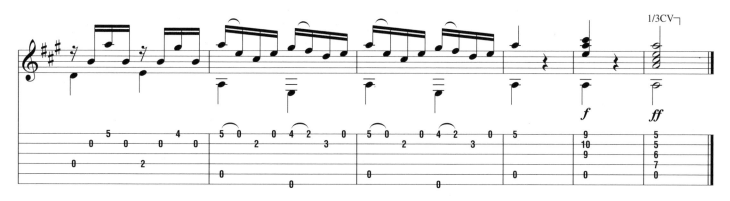

Vaghe belleze et bionde treccie d'oro vedi che per ti moro

Anonymous Italian 16th Century

Tuning:
(low to high) D-A-D-G-B-E

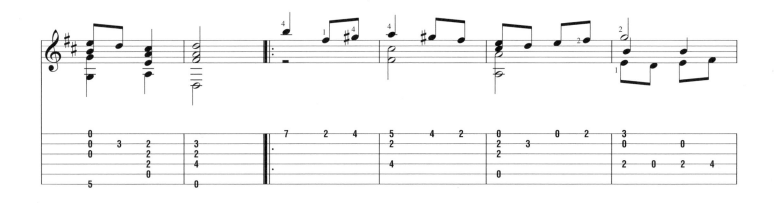

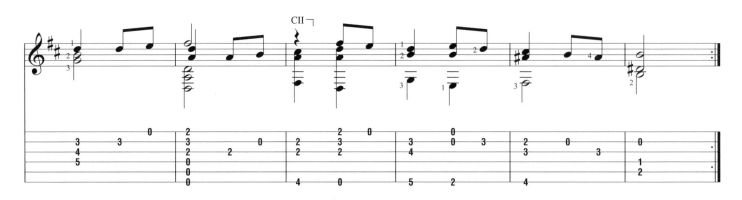